25 & 30HP EFI
QUICK. RELIABLE. EFFICIENT.

Mercury 25 and 30hp FourStroke outboards make light work of your biggest adventures. Quick and compact. Reliable and durable. Efficient and easy to own. FourStroke outboards bring big capabilities to small vessels.

- Exceptionally Smooth, Quiet and Efficient
- Outstanding Speed and Acceleration
- One of the lightest 3 cylinders in class
- Easy to start and reliable with Battery-free EFI (Electronic Fuel Injection)
- Exclusive Intuitive Tiller Handle
- SmartCraft Capable (Electric Start Models)
- 3+3=6 Year Fully transferable, non-declining Warranty*

*Terms and Conditions apply

mercurymarine.com.au

MERCURY
GO BOLDLY.

Contents

Fish Illustrations: Trevor Hawkins

Published in 2024 by
Australian Fishing Network Pty Ltd
PO Box 544, Croydon, VIC 3136
Tel: (03) 9729 8788   Email: sales@afn.com.au   www.afn.com.au

© Copyright Australian Fishing Network 2024   ISBN 9781 8651 3428 4

DISCLAIMER

The solar/lunar bite times in this book were derived from the program WXTide32 and are predictions. While they are as accurate as possible, they should be used as a guide only. Local conditions and changes can cause variations, so consult a website such as the Bureau of Meteorology Oceanographic Services, (www. bom.gov.au/oceanography/tides) as close as possible to the tide date and time before your fishing trip for the most up-to-date information and if you require certified information.

The publisher, Australian Fishing Network, advises that the information in this guide should not be used for navigation and should not be relied on for crucial situations.

Huk

AVAILABLE NOW

Tim Smith's Using Bite Times

'Solunar' theory suggests all creatures great and small respond in some way to the influences of both the Sun and the Moon during the course of a day.

This book lists the peak activity times along with the moon phases and it should become an indispensable tool for when you're planning a trip.

The peak activity times are presented in this book to simulate the logical progression of the Moon as it orbits the Earth. The first is the minor peak at moonrise, no *matter what time of day at which it occurs. The second the major peak when the moon is directly overhead, the third is the minor peak at moonset and the fourth is the major peak when the moon is directly overhead on the opposite side of the globe.*

Solunar (solar and lunar) theory is one of nature's mysteries which many of us find difficult to consider with any merit. A number of books, tables and articles have been written on the subject of lunar and solar influences on animal behaviour. Solunar theory suggests all creatures great and small respond in some way to the influences of both the Sun and the Moon during the course of a day. Specifically this response is often seen as an increase or decrease in activity level. Increased activity periods have often been referred to as peak or prime times.

The combination of centrifugal force produced by the Earth's rotation and the Moon's daily crossing of the sky generates our tides. Such enormous force is produced by these phenomena that it causes the Earth's surface to bulge up to 16 centimetres. Could lunar cycles impact on man? You be the judge. The human gestation period is 266 days, the average synodic interval between two consecutive new Moons is 29.530589 days; 266 divided by 29.530589 equals 9.008 lunar months. Sound familiar? Man is made up of approximately 80 per cent water. We know what happens tidally to huge bodies of water. Do you think there is a remote possibility that we too could unknowingly experience the effects of this heavenly sphere?

It is important to understand that what influences one creature may not influence another in any circumstance. For example there are a number of intertidal organisms that are most active when submerged by an incoming tide, creatures such as barnacles, green crabs, snails, clams, and oysters. Others, like soldier crabs and shorebirds, are especially adapted to feed on beaches exposed at low tide. The lower the creature's order in the animal kingdom the more likely it is to respond to solar and lunar stimuli.

LIGHT THEORY

The light theory suggests that light levels during the day and night dictate feeding activity times. For example it is said that fishing is better on the mornings immediately leading up to and following the period of new Moon because the fish have been unable to feed during the periods of low light during the night. Fishing is also said to be good during the nights leading up to and following the full Moon because of increased evening light levels.

SOLAR THEORY

To some extent the solar theory is reliant upon seasonal changes, therefore I have provided you with a brief summary of the seasonal patterns and how they influence the Southern Hemisphere.

The principle of the solar theory works on the various instances of the Sun's rise, upper transit, set, and lower transit to identify the peak activity periods. Following a long period of darkness the animal kingdom is given a kick-start to the day as dawn approaches. Many creatures stir from their rest period and warm with the Sun to commence the daily routine of food gathering. All animal life has a preferred temperature range and fish are no exception to this rule. It is said that seasonal conditions may dictate when particular fish species will commence to feed.

So although dawn and dusk have been historically noted as prime fishing times if we review the seasonal fluctuations in day and night time temperatures we may see cause for reassessing our reliance on these times. For example during the colder months peak feeding times may coincide during the warmest time of the day; just after midday when the water temperatures have increased to a more preferred level. Conversely, during the warmer months peak feeding times may align with the coolest times of the day; dusk 'til dawn.

SEASONS

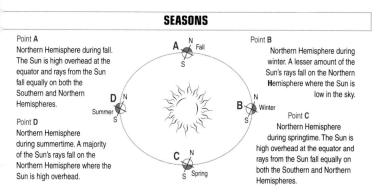

Point **A**
Northern Hemisphere during fall. The Sun is high overhead at the equator and rays from the Sun fall equally on both the Southern and Northern Hemispheres.

Point **B**
Northern Hemisphere during winter. A lesser amount of the Sun's rays fall on the Northern **H**emisphere where the Sun is low in the sky.

Point **D**
Northern Hemisphere during summertime. A majority of the Sun's rays fall on the Northern Hemisphere where the Sun is high overhead.

Point **C**
Northern Hemisphere during springtime. The Sun is high overhead at the equator and rays from the Sun fall equally on both the Southern and Northern Hemispheres.

LUNAR THEORY

To help you understand the lunar theory in more depth I have provided a brief outline of the various lunar phases. When you watch the Moon over a course of several days you will see that its appearance changes. The varying appearances called 'phases' depend upon the relative positions of the Sun and Moon.

MOON PHASES

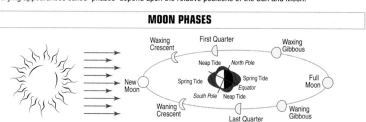

NEW MOON

When the Moon is between the Sun and the Earth we cannot see any of the illuminated side of the Moon, the Moon is dark, we call this phase the new Moon and it is the beginning of a new lunar month. The Moon rises and sets with the Sun during the new Moon. The gravitational forces exerted on the Earth by the Moon and the Sun is greatest at this time. The first of the spring tides for the lunar month occurs during this period.

FULL MOON

As the illuminated portion grows we have a waxing gibbous Moon. The full Moon occurs when the Moon reaches the side of the Earth opposite from the Sun. It appears large and bright. The Moon rises as the Sun is setting—it is overhead about midnight and sets close to dawn. The gravitational forces on the Earth have increased since the first quarter and now the combined pull of the Moon and the Sun is at a maximum again for the lunar month, the second of the spring tides occur.

FIRST QUARTER

The amount of lighted surface visible from the Earth begins to grow and we see a waxing crescent Moon. When the Moon reaches the first quarter we see half of it lit. The Moon rises during the middle of the day and is overhead about dusk and sets around midnight. The Moon's illuminated side will appear on the right in the Northern Hemisphere. The gravitational forces on the Earth have reduced since the new Moon and now the combined pull of the Moon and the Sun is at a minimum for the lunar month. The first of the neap tides for the Lunar month occurs at this time.

LAST QUARTER

The gravitational forces on the Earth have reduced since the full Moon and now the combined pull of the Moon and the Sun is at a minimum again for the lunar month. The second of the neap tides for the lunar month occurs at this time. As a waning crescent, the Moon diminishes to a thin sliver, returning to a new Moon after approximately 29.5 solar days or one lunar month. As the Moon revolves around the Earth it rotates on its own axis at the same rate it revolves, therefore the Moon always keeps the same face toward the Earth.

TIDAL FORCES

As the Earth rotates on its axis once every 24 hours relative to the Sun, and 24 hours and 53 minutes relative to the Moon; the Moon rises approximately 53 minutes later with respect to the Sun each day. This delay or lagging can be seen in the variation of tides from day to day.

The principle of the lunar theory works on the various instances of the Moon's rise, upper transit, set, and lower transit to identify the peak activity periods. This theory can also take into account the various lunar phases and the proximity (apogee and perigee) of the Moon to the Earth during the period of one lunation (new Moon to new Moon). Because the Moon orbits the Earth on an elliptical path, the distance between the two is always changing. The Moon has less gravitational influence on the Earth around the time of apogee when the distance between the two bodies is at a maximum. Greater gravitational influence occurs around the time of perigee when the distance between the Earth and the Moon is at a minimum.

SOLUNAR THEORY

Solunar theory accounts for the peaks associated with both the solar and lunar theories. It also incorporates the Sun's lower transit (midnight), and it also flags the coinciding times of peaks from the other theories. In other words it takes an each way bet on the three individual theories. Additionally the solunar theory recognises the gravitational effect on the Earth from the combined force produced by the Moon and the Sun in tandem. This gravitational force changes with the seasons, with the phases of the Moon, and with the Sun and Moon's proximity to Earth.

EFFECTS ON FISHING

Fishing wise, catch rates are often said to be higher around the new and full Moon phases. This makes sense when you consider the increased gravitational influence on the Earth during these periods. However this is further bolstered if you consider that during these times we are provided with three windows of peak activity level during general daylight hours, each coinciding with dawn, noon, or dusk. Around the period of new Moon, the Moon is in harmony with the Sun, they rise, transit and set together. During the period of full Moon, the Moon and Sun directly oppose each other, the Moon sets when the Sun rises, the Moon is underfoot at noon, and the Moon rises at Sun set. Whether or not the increased activity levels in lower organisms is the catalyst for larger and perhaps predatory creatures to begin feeding is arguable. Your observations will also show increased activity levels in the non predatory herbivore family during the peak times.

FEEDING PATTERNS

Does activity occur outside of these peak periods? Of course. Remember not all species will react in an identical manner during the peak times. The bottom line is fish don't always feel hungry! They follow certain feeding patterns but aren't totally immune to sampling the odd tid-bit throughout the course of the day. As with most creatures, strength is gained through struggle; and only the fittest and strongest survive in the wild. While minimum work for maximum return is the hallmark of big fish, a fish's condition and health must also be maintained through foraging for food. Natural rhythms aside, fish are also subject to local conditions such as the various fluctuations in air temperature, barometric pressure, water levels, water clarity, and water temperature. These should all be considered when using the tables.

 BITE TIME ADJUSTMENTS (Minutes)

Approximate variation times only, taken from various sources.

Albury	-5	Eden	-20	Newcastle	-30
Armadale	-30	Eucumbene	-20	Nowra	-25
Batemans Bay	-25	Glen Innes	-30	Parkes	-10
Bega	-25	Goulburn	-10	Port Macquarie	-30
Bermagui	-20	Grafton	-30	Port Stephens	-30
Bourke	0	Griffith	0	Seal Rocks	-30
Braidwood	-10	Hat Head	-30	Snowy Mountains	-20
Broken Hill	+10	Jervis Bay	-20	Sydney	-30
Canberra	-10	Lithgow	-25	Tweed Heads	-30
Coffs Harbour	-30	Menindee Lakes	+10	Wagga Wagga	-5
Corryong	-10	Moree	-15	Wollongong	-30
Dubbo	-10	Narrandera	-5	Yamba	-30

TIDE

TIMES

Tim Smith's

POPULAR TIDE ADJUSTMENTS

Ballina Boat Dock	+15min	Morpeth	+3hrs 10min
Batemans Bay	-1min	Moruya	+30min
Bermagui	+5min	Murwillumbah	+2hrs 30min
Blackmans Point	+1hr 15min	Narooma	+40min
Botany Bay	+3min	Nelson Bay	+30min
Broughton Island	-6min	Peats Ferry Bridge	+1hr
Byron Bay	0	Pindimar	+45min
Chinderah	+1hr 15min	Pittwater Entrance	0
Clyde River Bridge	+15min	Port Hacking	+2min
Coffs Harbour	-2min	Port Hacking Audley	+30min
Como	+30min	Port Hacking Burraneer	+15min
Coraki	+4hrs	Port Hacking Lilli Pilli	+30min
Crookhaven Jetty	+15min	Port Macquarie	+21min
Crowdy Head	0	Port Stephens	0
Danger Island	+18min	Queens Lake	+2hrs
Dolls Point	+15min	Raleigh	+1hr
Ettalong	+30min	Raymond Terrace	+1hr 55min
Evans Head Bridge	0	Salamander Bay	+45min
Fig Tree Bridge	+15min	Sandon	+30min
Forster	+1min	Shoalhaven Riv' Nowra	+2hrs 10min
Gabo Island	-9min	Shoalhaven Riv'O'Keefes Pt	+2hrs
Gladesville Bridge	+15min	Silverwater Bridge	+15min
Gladstone	+2hrs 10min	Soldiers Point	+1hr
Grafton	+4hrs 1 min	South West Rocks	+1hr 2min
Greenwell Point	+45min	Swansea	-3min
Harrington	+1 min	Taree	+2hrs
Harrington Inlet	+16min	Tea Gardens	+1hr
Hexham	+1hr 10min	Terranora Inlet	+2hrs 10min
Huskisson	+3min	The Spit Bridge	0
Iluka	0	Trial Bay	0
Jervis Bay	-3min	Tweed Heads	+4min
Kempsey	+3hrs 15min	Ulladulla Harbour	0
Kendall	+3hrs 30min	Ulmarra	+4hrs 30min
Kiama	0	Wardell	+1 hr 30 min
Kurnell	0	Watson Taylors Lake	+2hrs
Lismore	+1hr 15min	Wauchope	+1hr 30min
Liverpool+	+2hrs 30min	Windsor	+5hrs 50min
Lower Portland Ferry	+3hrs 5min	Wingham	+3hrs 15min
Lugarno	+1hr	Wisemans Ferry	+2hrs 15min
Maclean	+2hrs 15min	Wollomba River mouth	+1hr 50min
Merimbula Lake Bridge	+1hr 30min	Wollongong	0
Milperra	+2hrs 10min	Wooli	+1hr 5min

Day	Date		Tide 1	
Sun	1		1:25 AM	(0.39) L
Mon	2		1:57 AM	(0.37) L
Tue	3	●	2:27 AM	(0.36) L
Wed	4		2:54 AM	(0.36) L
THu	5		3:21 AM	(0.38) L
Fri	6		3:47 AM	(0.41) L
Sat	7		4:15 AM	(0.45) L
Sun	8		4:44 AM	(0.50) L
Mon	9		5:15 AM	(0.57) L
Tue	10		12:07 AM	(1.20) H
Wed	11		1:06 AM	(1.12) H
THu	12		2:23 AM	(1.08) H
Fri	13		3:49 AM	(1.09) H
Sat	14		4:59 AM	(1.17) H
Sun	15		5:51 AM	(1.28) H
Mon	16		12:39 AM	(0.27) L
Tue	17		1:20 AM	(0.17) L
Wed	18	○	2:01 AM	(0.12) L
THu	19		2:43 AM	(0.12) L
Fri	20		3:23 AM	(0.17) L
Sat	21		4:04 AM	(0.26) L
Sun	22		4:47 AM	(0.38) L
Mon	23		5:32 AM	(0.51) L
Tue	24		12:51 AM	(1.20) H
Wed	25		2:09 AM	(1.11) H
THu	26		3:36 AM	(1.10) H
Fri	27		4:46 AM	(1.15) H
Sat	28		5:36 AM	(1.23) H
Sun	29		12:14 AM	(0.45) L
Mon	30		12:47 AM	(0.42) L

SEPTEMBER 2024

Tide 2		Tide 3		Tide 4	
7:20 AM	(1.31) **H**	12:56 PM	(0.52) L	7:21 PM	(1.72) **H**
7:55 AM	(1.37) **H**	1:35 PM	(0.48) L	7:57 PM	(1.71) **H**
8:27 AM	(1.41) **H**	2:12 PM	(0.46) L	8:30 PM	(1.69) **H**
8:59 AM	(1.44) **H**	2:47 PM	(0.46) L	9:01 PM	(1.65) **H**
9:30 AM	(1.47) **H**	3:24 PM	(0.47) L	9:33 PM	(1.58) **H**
10:01 AM	(1.50) **H**	4:01 PM	(0.50) L	10:07 PM	(1.50) **H**
10:34 AM	(1.51) **H**	4:43 PM	(0.53) L	10:43 PM	(1.40) **H**
11:10 AM	(1.51) **H**	5:27 PM	(0.58) L	11:21 PM	(1.30) **H**
11:50 AM	(1.49) **H**	6:18 PM	(0.63) L		
5:54 AM	(0.63) L	12:37 PM	(1.47) **H**	7:21 PM	(0.67) L
6:44 AM	(0.70) L	1:35 PM	(1.45) **H**	8:40 PM	(0.67) L
7:52 AM	(0.73) L	2:46 PM	(1.47) **H**	10:00 PM	(0.61) L
9:12 AM	(0.71) L	4:00 PM	(1.54) **H**	11:03 PM	(0.51) L
10:24 AM	(0.64) L	5:02 PM	(1.66) **H**	11:54 PM	(0.39) L
11:24 AM	(0.53) L	5:56 PM	(1.78) **H**		
6:37 AM	(1.40) **H**	12:18 PM	(0.41) L	6:45 PM	(1.88) **H**
7:22 AM	(1.53) **H**	1:10 PM	(0.30) L	7:32 PM	(1.93) **H**
8:06 AM	(1.64) **H**	2:01 PM	(0.23) L	8:20 PM	(1.91) **H**
8:51 AM	(1.73) **H**	2:55 PM	(0.19) L	9:09 PM	(1.83) **H**
9:37 AM	(1.80) **H**	3:49 PM	(0.21) L	9:59 PM	(1.69) **H**
10:24 AM	(1.81) **H**	4:45 PM	(0.26) L	10:51 PM	(1.52) **H**
11:14 AM	(1.79) **H**	5:47 PM	(0.35) L	11:47 PM	(1.34) **H**
12:06 PM	(1.73) **H**	6:56 PM	(0.44) L		
6:25 AM	(0.62) L	1:05 PM	(1.64) **H**	8:13 PM	(0.51) L
7:30 AM	(0.71) L	2:15 PM	(1.57) **H**	9:32 PM	(0.53) L
8:49 AM	(0.74) L	3:32 PM	(1.54) **H**	10:42 PM	(0.52) L
10:04 AM	(0.71) L	4:40 PM	(1.54) **H**	11:33 PM	(0.49) L
11:07 AM	(0.65) L	5:32 PM	(1.57) **H**		
6:16 AM	(1.31) **H**	11:58 AM	(0.58) L	6:15 PM	(1.59) **H**
6:51 AM	(1.38) **H**	12:40 PM	(0.52) L	6:53 PM	(1.60) **H**

SOLAR/LUNAR

BITE TIMES

Tim Smith's

Apogee moon phase on Friday 6th
Perigee moon phase on Wednesday 18th
● **New moon on Tuesday 3rd**
First quarter moon on Wednesday 11th
○ **Full moon on Wednesday 18th**
Last quarter moon phase on Wednesday 25th

Sydney, NSW: Rise: 05:50am Set: 05:40pm
(Note: These sun rise/set times are averages for the month)

DAY	MINOR BITE	MAJOR BITE	MINOR BITE	MAJOR BITE	SALT WATER RATING	FRESH WATER RATING
SUN 1	4:57 AM	9:58 AM	3:06 PM	10:19 PM	6	7
MON 2	5:25 AM	10:42 AM	4:07 PM	11:03 PM	8	8
TUE 3	5:49 AM	11:24 AM	5:07 PM	11:43 PM	● 8	8
WED 4	6:10 AM	12:03 PM	6:05 PM		8	6
THUR 5	6:31 AM	12:42 PM	7:03 PM	12:22 AM	7	6
FRI 6	6:51 AM	1:21 PM	8:01 PM	1:01 AM	6	7
SAT 7	7:13 AM	2:01 PM	9:00 PM	1:41 AM	6	7
SUN 8	7:37 AM	2:44 PM	10:01 PM	2:22 AM	5	5
MON 9	8:05 AM	3:29 PM	11:03 PM	3:06 AM	4	6
TUE 10	8:38 AM	4:19 PM		3:53 AM	3	5
WED 11	9:20 AM	5:12 PM	12:07 AM	4:45 AM	4	6

DAY	MINOR BITE	MAJOR BITE	MINOR BITE	MAJOR BITE	SALT WATER RATING	FRESH WATER RATING
THUR 12	10:11 AM	6:09 PM	1:09 AM	5:40 AM	5	6
FRI 13	11:12 AM	7:07 PM	2:06 AM	6:38 AM	4	5
SAT 14	12:21 PM	8:06 PM	2:57 AM	7:36 AM	3	5
SUN 15	1:36 PM	9:02 PM	3:40 AM	8:33 AM	6	6
MON 16	2:53 PM	9:57 PM	4:16 AM	9:29 AM	5	7
TUE 17	4:10 PM	10:49 PM	4:48 AM	10:22 AM	3	8
WED 18	5:26 PM	11:41 PM	5:16 AM	11:15 AM	◯ 5	7
THUR 19	6:43 PM		5:44 AM	12:07 PM	7	6
FRI 20	7:59 PM	12:33 AM	6:12 AM	12:59 PM	7	6
SAT 21	9:17 PM	1:26 AM	6:42 AM	1:53 PM	5	5
SUN 22	10:33 PM	2:21 AM	7:18 AM	2:50 PM	4	4
MON 23	11:44 PM	3:19 AM	8:00 AM	3:48 PM	3	6
TUE 24		4:18 AM	8:49 AM	4:47 PM	4	4
WED 25	12:48 AM	5:17 AM	9:46 AM	5:45 PM	5	5
THUR 26	1:42 AM	6:14 AM	10:49 AM	6:40 PM	6	6
FRI 27	2:25 AM	7:07 AM	11:54 AM	7:31 PM	7	7
SAT 28	3:01 AM	7:56 AM	12:58 PM	8:18 PM	7	8
SUN 29	3:29 AM	8:41 AM	2:01 PM	9:02 PM	5	8
MON 30	3:54 AM	9:23 AM	3:01 PM	9:42 PM	6	7

TIDE TIMES

Tim Smith's

Fort Denison

Day	Date		Tide 1	
Tue	1		1:17 AM	(0.40) L
Wed	2		1:45 AM	(0.38) L
THu	3	●	2:11 AM	(0.39) L
Fri	4		2:36 AM	(0.41) L
Sat	5		3:03 AM	(0.44) L
Sun	6		4:31 AM	(0.49) L
Mon	7		5:02 AM	(0.55) L
Tue	8		12:03 AM	(1.24) H
Wed	9		12:51 AM	(1.17) H
THu	10		1:52 AM	(1.12) H
Fri	11		3:07 AM	(1.10) H
Sat	12		4:27 AM	(1.15) H
Sun	13		5:31 AM	(1.25) H
Mon	14		12:16 AM	(0.35) L
Tue	15		1:01 AM	(0.26) L
Wed	16		1:44 AM	(0.19) L
THu	17	○	2:25 AM	(0.18) L
Fri	18		3:06 AM	(0.21) L
Sat	19		3:48 AM	(0.28) L
Sun	20		4:31 AM	(0.37) L
Mon	21		5:16 AM	(0.48) L
Tue	22		12:37 AM	(1.26) H
Wed	23		1:41 AM	(1.17) H
THu	24		2:54 AM	(1.13) H
Fri	25		4:08 AM	(1.15) H
Sat	26		5:10 AM	(1.21) H
Sun	27		5:59 AM	(1.28) H
Mon	28		12:25 AM	(0.50) L
Tue	29		12:59 AM	(0.48) L
Wed	30		1:30 AM	(0.45) L
THu	31		1:58 AM	(0.45) L

POPULAR TIDE ADJUSTMENTS

Ballina Boat Dock	+15min	Morpeth	+3hrs 10min
Batemans Bay	-1min	Moruya	+30min
Bermagui	+5min	Murwillumbah	+2hrs 30min
Blackmans Point	+1hr 15min	Narooma	+40min
Botany Bay	+3min	Nelson Bay	+30min
Broughton Island	-6min	Peats Ferry Bridge	+1hr
Byron Bay	0	Pindimar	+45min
Chinderah	+1hr 15min	Pittwater Entrance	0
Clyde River Bridge	+15min	Port Hacking	+2min
Coffs Harbour	-2min	Port Hacking Audley	+ 30min
Como	+30min	Port Hacking Burraneer	+15min
Coraki	+4hrs	Port Hacking Lilli Pilli	+30min
Crookhaven Jetty	+15min	Port Macquarie	+21min
Crowdy Head	0	Port Stephens	0
Danger Island	+18min	Queens Lake	+2hrs
Dolls Point	+15min	Raleigh	+1hr
Ettalong	+30min	Raymond Terrace	+1hr 55min
Evans Head Bridge	0	Salamander Bay	+45min
Fig Tree Bridge	+15min	Sandon	+30min
Forster	+1min	Shoalhaven Riv' Nowra	+2hrs 10min
Gabo Island	-9min	Shoalhaven Riv'O'Keefes Pt	+2hrs
Gladesville Bridge	+15min	Silverwater Bridge	+15min
Gladstone	+3min	Soldiers Point	+1hr
Grafton	+4hrs 1 min	South West Rocks	+1hr 2min
Greenwell Point	+45min	Swansea	-3min
Harrington	+1 min	Taree	+2hrs
Harrington Inlet	+16min	Tea Gardens	+1hr
Hexham	+1hr 10min	Terranora Inlet	+2hrs 10min
Huskisson	+3min	The Spit Bridge	0
Iluka	0	Trial Bay	0
Jervis Bay	-3min	Tweed Heads	+4min
Kempsey	+3hrs 15min	Ulladulla Harbour	0
Kendall	+3hrs 30min	Ulmarra	+4hrs 30min
Kiama	0	Wardell	+1 hr 30 min
Kurnell	0	Watson Taylors Lake	+2hrs
Lismore	+1hr 15min	Wauchope	+1hr 30min
Liverpool+	+2hrs 30min	Windsor	+5hrs 50min
Lower Portland Ferry	+3hrs 5min	Wingham	+3hrs 15min
Lugarno	+1hr	Wisemans Ferry	+2hrs 15min
Maclean	+2hrs 15min	Wollomba River mouth	+1hr 50min
Merimbula Lake Bridge	+1hr 30min	Wollongong	0
Milperra	+2hrs 10min	Wooli	+1hr 5min

Tide 2		Tide 3		Tide 4	
7:24 AM	(1.45) H	1:17 PM	(0.48) L	7:27 PM	(1.59) H
7:54 AM	(1.51) H	1:54 PM	(0.44) L	8:00 PM	(1.57) H
8:24 AM	(1.56) H	2:30 PM	(0.43) L	8:33 PM	(1.53) H
8:54 AM	(1.60) H	3:06 PM	(0.42) L	9:07 PM	(1.47) H
9:25 AM	(1.62) H	3:45 PM	(0.44) L	9:43 PM	(1.40) H
10:58 AM	(1.63) H	5:25 PM	(0.47) L	11:21 PM	(1.32) H
11:33 AM	(1.61) H	6:08 PM	(0.51) L		
5:37 AM	(0.61) L	12:14 PM	(1.58) H	6:59 PM	(0.56) L
6:19 AM	(0.67) L	1:01 PM	(1.54) H	8:00 PM	(0.60) L
7:15 AM	(0.73) L	2:00 PM	(1.50) H	9:12 PM	(0.60) L
8:27 AM	(0.75) L	3:12 PM	(1.51) H	10:25 PM	(0.54) L
9:48 AM	(0.72) L	4:27 PM	(1.56) H	11:26 PM	(0.45) L
11:02 AM	(0.63) L	5:32 PM	(1.65) H		
6:23 AM	(1.38) H	12:06 PM	(0.51) L	6:28 PM	(1.73) H
7:09 AM	(1.53) H	1:02 PM	(0.39) L	7:19 PM	(1.79) H
7:54 AM	(1.67) H	1:58 PM	(0.28) L	8:10 PM	(1.79) H
8:39 AM	(1.80) H	2:51 PM	(0.20) L	9:00 PM	(1.74) H
9:24 AM	(1.89) H	3:45 PM	(0.17) L	9:51 PM	(1.64) H
10:11 AM	(1.94) H	4:41 PM	(0.18) L	10:45 PM	(1.51) H
10:59 AM	(1.93) H	5:37 PM	(0.23) L	11:39 PM	(1.38) H
11:48 AM	(1.87) H	6:37 PM	(0.32) L		
6:06 AM	(0.59) L	12:41 PM	(1.77) H	7:41 PM	(0.41) L
7:01 AM	(0.69) L	1:38 PM	(1.66) H	8:50 PM	(0.49) L
8:08 AM	(0.75) L	2:44 PM	(1.56) H	9:58 PM	(0.53) L
9:23 AM	(0.77) L	3:55 PM	(1.49) H	10:57 PM	(0.55) L
10:36 AM	(0.75) L	5:00 PM	(1.47) H	11:45 PM	(0.53) L
11:39 AM	(0.70) L	5:53 PM	(1.47) H		
6:39 AM	(1.37) H	12:32 PM	(0.63) L	6:38 PM	(1.47) H
7:15 AM	(1.46) H	1:17 PM	(0.57) L	7:17 PM	(1.47) H
7:47 AM	(1.53) H	1:59 PM	(0.51) L	7:55 PM	(1.46) H
8:19 AM	(1.61) H	2:36 PM	(0.46) L	8:31 PM	(1.45) H

SOLAR/LUNAR
BITE TIMES

Tim Smith's

Apogee moon phase on Thursday 3rd and Wednesday 30th
Perigee moon phase on Thursday 17th
● **New moon on Thursday 3rd**
First quarter moon on Friday 11th
○ **Full moon on Thursday 17th**
Last quarter moon phase on Thursday 24th

Sydney, NSW: Rise: 06:13am Set: 07:08pm

Note: Daylight Savings start (clocks turn forward 1 hour) on Sunday, October 1st at 2:00 AM.
Subtract 1 hour to rise/set time for days before October 1st. These sun rise/set times are averages for the month

DAY	MINOR BITE	MAJOR BITE	MINOR BITE	MAJOR BITE	SALT WATER RATING	FRESH WATER RATING
TUE 1	4:16 AM	10:03 AM	3:59 PM	10:22 PM	8	8
WED 2	4:37 AM	10:42 AM	4:57 PM	11:01 PM	8	8
THUR 3	4:57 AM	11:21 AM	5:54 PM	11:40 PM	● 8	8
FRI 4	5:18 AM	12:00 PM	6:53 PM		8	6
SAT 5	5:41 AM	12:42 PM	7:53 PM	12:21 AM	7	6
SUN 6	6:07 AM	1:26 PM	8:55 PM	1:03 AM	6	7
MON 7	6:39 AM	2:14 PM	9:58 PM	1:49 AM	5	5
TUE 8	7:17 AM	3:06 PM	11:00 PM	2:39 AM	4	6
WED 9	8:04 AM	4:00 PM	11:58 PM	3:32 AM	3	5
THUR 10	9:00 AM	4:57 PM		4:28 AM	3	5
FRI 11	10:04 AM	5:53 PM	12:50 AM	5:25 AM	4	6

DAY	MINOR BITE	MAJOR BITE	MINOR BITE	MAJOR BITE	SALT WATER RATING	FRESH WATER RATING
SAT 12	11:14 AM	6:49 PM	1:34 AM	6:20 AM	5	6
SUN 13	12:28 PM	7:42 PM	2:12 AM	7:15 AM	4	5
MON 14	1:42 PM	8:34 PM	2:44 AM	8:07 AM	3	5
TUE 15	2:57 PM	9:25 PM	3:13 AM	8:59 AM	6	6
WED 16	4:13 PM	10:16 PM	3:41 AM	9:50 AM	3	8
THUR 17	5:30 PM	11:09 PM	4:08 AM	10:42 AM	◯ 5	7
FRI 18	6:48 PM		4:37 AM	11:36 AM	7	6
SAT 19	8:08 PM	12:04 AM	5:11 AM	12:33 PM	7	6
SUN 20	9:24 PM	1:03 AM	5:51 AM	1:33 PM	5	5
MON 21	10:35 PM	2:04 AM	6:38 AM	2:34 PM	4	4
TUE 22	11:35 PM	3:05 AM	7:35 AM	3:35 PM	3	6
WED 23		4:05 AM	8:38 AM	4:33 PM	4	4
THUR 24	12:23 AM	5:01 AM	9:44 AM	5:26 PM	5	5
FRI 25	1:02 AM	5:52 AM	10:49 AM	6:15 PM	6	6
SAT 26	1:33 AM	6:39 AM	11:53 AM	7:00 PM	6	6
SUN 27	1:59 AM	7:22 AM	12:54 PM	7:42 PM	7	7
MON 28	2:21 AM	8:03 AM	1:52 PM	8:22 PM	7	8
TUE 29	2:42 AM	8:42 AM	2:50 PM	9:00 PM	5	8
WED 30	3:03 AM	9:20 AM	3:48 PM	9:40 PM	6	7
THUR 31	3:23 AM	10:00 AM	4:46 PM	10:20 PM	8	8

TIDE TIMES

Tim Smith's

POPULAR TIDE ADJUSTMENTS

Ballina Boat Dock	+15min	Morpeth	+3hrs 10min
Batemans Bay	-1min	Moruya	+30min
Bermagui	+5min	Murwillumbah	+2hrs 30min
Blackmans Point	+1hr 15min	Narooma	+40min
Botany Bay	+3min	Nelson Bay	+30min
Broughton Island	-6min	Peats Ferry Bridge	+1hr
Byron Bay	0	Pindimar	+45min
Chinderah	+1hr 15min	Pittwater Entrance	0
Clyde River Bridge	+15min	Port Hacking	+2min
Coffs Harbour	-2min	Port Hacking Audley	+ 30min
Como	+30min	Port Hacking Burraneer	+15min
Coraki	+4hrs	Port Hacking Lilli Pilli	+30min
Crookhaven Jetty	+15min	Port Macquarie	+21min
Crowdy Head	0	Port Stephens	0
Danger Island	+18min	Queens Lake	+2hrs
Dolls Point	+15min	Raleigh	+1hr
Ettalong	+30min	Raymond Terrace	+1hr 55min
Evans Head Bridge	0	Salamander Bay	+45min
Fig Tree Bridge	+15min	Sandon	+30min
Forster	+1min	Shoalhaven Riv' Nowra	+2hrs 10min
Gabo Island	-9min	Shoalhaven Riv'O'Keefes Pt	+2hrs
Gladesville Bridge	+15min	Silverwater Bridge	+15min
Gladstone	+2hrs 10min	Soldiers Point	+1hr
Grafton	+4hrs 1 min	South West Rocks	+1hr 2min
Greenwell Point	+45min	Swansea	-3min
Harrington	+1 min	Taree	+2hrs
Harrington Inlet	+16min	Tea Gardens	+1hr
Hexham	+1hr 10min	Terranora Inlet	+2hrs 10min
Huskisson	+3min	The Spit Bridge	0
Iluka	0	Trial Bay	0
Jervis Bay	-3min	Tweed Heads	+4min
Kempsey	+3hrs 15min	Ulladulla Harbour	0
Kendall	+3hrs 30min	Ulmarra	+4hrs 30min
Kiama	0	Wardell	+1 hr 30 min
Kurnell	0	Watson Taylors Lake	+2hrs
Lismore	+1hr 15min	Wauchope	+1hr 30min
Liverpool+	+2hrs 30min	Windsor	+5hrs 50min
Lower Portland Ferry	+3hrs 5min	Wingham	+3hrs 15min
Lugarno	+1hr	Wisemans Ferry	+2hrs 15min
Maclean	+2hrs 15min	Wollomba River mouth	+1hr 50min
Merimbula Lake Bridge	+1hr 30min	Wollongong	0
Milperra	+2hrs 10min	Wooli	+1hr 5min

Day	Date		Tide 1	
Fri	1	●	2:26 AM	(0.45) L
Sat	2		2:55 AM	(0.48) L
Sun	3		3:25 AM	(0.51) L
Mon	4		3:58 AM	(0.55) L
Tue	5		4:34 AM	(0.59) L
Wed	6		5:15 AM	(0.64) L
THu	7		12:43 AM	(1.19) **H**
Fri	8		1:41 AM	(1.17) **H**
Sat	9		2:49 AM	(1.19) **H**
Sun	10		3:58 AM	(1.25) **H**
Mon	11		4:59 AM	(1.36) **H**
Tue	12		5:51 AM	(1.50) **H**
Wed	13		12:21 AM	(0.31) L
THu	14		1:05 AM	(0.29) L
Fri	15		1:49 AM	(0.30) L
Sat	16	○	2:33 AM	(0.34) L
Sun	17		3:18 AM	(0.40) L
Mon	18		4:05 AM	(0.48) L
Tue	19		4:53 AM	(0.55) L
Wed	20		12:22 AM	(1.25) **H**
THu	21		1:19 AM	(1.21) **H**
Fri	22		2:18 AM	(1.19) **H**
Sat	23		3:19 AM	(1.21) **H**
Sun	24		4:16 AM	(1.26) **H**
Mon	25		5:07 AM	(1.33) **H**
Tue	26		5:52 AM	(1.41) **H**
Wed	27		12:01 AM	(0.54) L
THu	28		12:38 AM	(0.53) L
Fri	29		1:12 AM	(0.53) L
Sat	30		1:45 AM	(0.53) L

NOVEMBER 2024

Tide 2		Tide 3		Tide 4	
8:50 AM	(1.67) **H**	3:14 PM	(0.43) L	9:08 PM	(1.41) **H**
9:22 AM	(1.71) **H**	3:51 PM	(0.41) L	9:45 PM	(1.37) **H**
9:55 AM	(1.73) **H**	4:30 PM	(0.41) L	10:25 PM	(1.33) **H**
10:30 AM	(1.74) **H**	5:11 PM	(0.42) L	11:06 PM	(1.28) **H**
11:09 AM	(1.72) **H**	5:55 PM	(0.46) L	11:51 PM	(1.23) **H**
11:52 AM	(1.68) **H**	6:45 PM	(0.49) L		
6:02 AM	(0.69) L	12:41 PM	(1.64) **H**	7:43 PM	(0.52) L
7:00 AM	(0.72) L	1:37 PM	(1.60) **H**	8:45 PM	(0.51) L
8:10 AM	(0.73) L	2:43 PM	(1.58) **H**	9:48 PM	(0.47) L
9:26 AM	(0.71) L	3:53 PM	(1.59) **H**	10:45 PM	(0.41) L
10:40 AM	(0.63) L	4:59 PM	(1.61) **H**	11:34 PM	(0.35) L
11:47 AM	(0.53) L	5:59 PM	(1.63) **H**		
6:40 AM	(1.65) **H**	12:49 PM	(0.41) L	6:55 PM	(1.63) **H**
7:27 AM	(1.79) **H**	1:48 PM	(0.31) L	7:50 PM	(1.60) **H**
8:14 AM	(1.91) **H**	2:45 PM	(0.23) L	8:44 PM	(1.54) **H**
9:01 AM	(1.98) **H**	3:39 PM	(0.19) L	9:38 PM	(1.47) **H**
9:49 AM	(2.00) **H**	4:33 PM	(0.20) L	10:33 PM	(1.39) **H**
10:38 AM	(1.97) **H**	5:27 PM	(0.25) L	11:28 PM	(1.31) **H**
11:28 AM	(1.90) **H**	6:21 PM	(0.32) L		
5:44 AM	(0.63) L	12:17 PM	(1.80) **H**	7:17 PM	(0.41) L
6:38 AM	(0.70) L	1:08 PM	(1.68) **H**	8:13 PM	(0.49) L
7:37 AM	(0.75) L	2:02 PM	(1.56) **H**	9:07 PM	(0.54) L
8:42 AM	(0.78) L	3:00 PM	(1.47) **H**	9:57 PM	(0.57) L
9:50 AM	(0.79) L	4:00 PM	(1.40) **H**	10:43 PM	(0.57) L
10:57 AM	(0.76) L	4:58 PM	(1.37) **H**	11:24 PM	(0.56) L
11:59 AM	(0.71) L	5:50 PM	(1.35) **H**		
6:32 AM	(1.50) **H**	12:51 PM	(0.64) L	6:38 PM	(1.34) **H**
7:10 AM	(1.59) **H**	1:38 PM	(0.56) L	7:23 PM	(1.34) **H**
7:45 AM	(1.66) **H**	2:19 PM	(0.50) L	8:06 PM	(1.33) **H**
8:20 AM	(1.73) **H**	2:59 PM	(0.44) L	8:47 PM	(1.32) **H**

SOLAR/LUNAR
BITE TIMES

Tim Smith's

Apogee moon phase on Tuesday 26th
Perigee moon phase on Thursday 14th
● New moon on Friday 1st
First quarter moon on Saturday 9th
○ Full moon on Saturday 16th
Last quarter moon phase on Saturday 23rd

Sydney, NSW: Rise: 05:40am Set: 07:30pm
(Note: These sun rise/set times are averages for the month)

DAY	MINOR BITE	MAJOR BITE	MINOR BITE	MAJOR BITE	SALT WATER RATING	FRESH WATER RATING
FRI 1	3:46 AM	10:41 AM	5:46 PM	11:02 PM	● 8	8
SAT 2	4:11 AM	11:24 AM	6:48 PM	11:48 PM	8	8
SUN 3	4:41 AM	12:12 PM	7:51 PM		8	6
MON 4	5:17 AM	1:02 PM	8:53 PM	12:37 AM	7	6
TUE 5	6:01 AM	1:56 PM	9:53 PM	1:29 AM	6	7
WED 6	6:54 AM	2:51 PM	10:46 PM	2:23 AM	5	5
THUR 7	7:55 AM	3:47 PM	11:32 PM	3:19 AM	4	6
FRI 8	9:02 AM	4:42 PM		4:14 AM	3	5
SAT 9	10:13 AM	5:34 PM	12:11 AM	5:08 AM	4	6
SUN 10	11:24 AM	6:25 PM	12:44 AM	5:59 AM	5	6
MON 11	12:36 PM	7:14 PM	1:13 AM	6:49 AM	4	5

DAY	MINOR BITE	MAJOR BITE	MINOR BITE	MAJOR BITE	SALT WATER RATING	FRESH WATER RATING
TUE 12	1:48 PM	8:03 PM	1:39 AM	7:38 AM	3	5
WED 13	3:02 PM	8:53 PM	2:06 AM	8:28 AM	6	6
THUR 14	4:18 PM	9:46 PM	2:33 AM	9:19 AM	5	7
FRI 15	5:36 PM	10:42 PM	3:04 AM	10:13 AM	3	8
SAT 16	6:55 PM	11:43 PM	3:40 AM	11:12 AM	○ 5	7
SUN 17	8:11 PM		4:24 AM	12:14 PM	7	6
MON 18	9:18 PM	12:46 AM	5:18 AM	1:16 PM	7	6
TUE 19	10:13 PM	1:48 AM	6:19 AM	2:18 PM	5	5
WED 20	10:58 PM	2:48 AM	7:27 AM	3:15 PM	4	4
THUR 21	11:32 PM	3:43 AM	8:35 AM	4:07 PM	3	6
FRI 22		4:33 AM	9:41 AM	4:55 PM	4	4
SAT 23	12:01 AM	5:18 AM	10:44 AM	5:38 PM	5	5
SUN 24	12:25 AM	6:00 AM	11:44 AM	6:19 PM	6	6
MON 25	12:47 AM	6:40 AM	12:42 PM	6:59 PM	7	7
TUE 26	1:07 AM	7:19 AM	1:39 PM	7:38 PM	7	8
WED 27	1:28 AM	7:58 AM	2:37 PM	8:18 PM	7	8
THUR 28	1:49 AM	8:38 AM	3:37 PM	8:59 PM	5	8
FRI 29	2:14 AM	9:21 AM	4:38 PM	9:44 PM	6	7
SAT 30	2:42 AM	10:07 AM	5:41 PM	10:32 PM	8	8

TIDE TIMES

Tim Smith's

POPULAR TIDE ADJUSTMENTS

Ballina Boat Dock	+15min	Morpeth	+3hrs 10min
Batemans Bay	-1min	Moruya	+30min
Bermagui	+5min	Murwillumbah	+2hrs 30min
Blackmans Point	+1hr 15min	Narooma	+40min
Botany Bay	+3min	Nelson Bay	+30min
Broughton Island	-6min	Peats Ferry Bridge	+1hr
Byron Bay	0	Pindimar	+45min
Chinderah	+1hr 15min	Pittwater Entrance	0
Clyde River Bridge	+15min	Port Hacking	+2min
Coffs Harbour	-2min	Port Hacking Audley	+ 30min
Como	+30min	Port Hacking Burraneer	+15min
Coraki	+4hrs	Port Hacking Lilli Pilli	+30min
Crookhaven Jetty	+15min	Port Macquarie	+21min
Crowdy Head	0	Port Stephens	0
Danger Island	+18min	Queens Lake	+2hrs
Dolls Point	+15min	Raleigh	+1hr
Ettalong	+30min	Raymond Terrace	+1hr 55min
Evans Head Bridge	0	Salamander Bay	+45min
Fig Tree Bridge	+15min	Sandon	+30min
Forster	+1min	Shoalhaven Riv' Nowra	+2hrs 10min
Gabo Island	-9min	Shoalhaven Riv'O'Keefes Pt	+2hrs
Gladesville Bridge	+15min	Silverwater Bridge	+15min
Gladstone	+2hrs 10min	Soldiers Point	+1hr
Grafton	+4hrs 1 min	South West Rocks	+1hr 2min
Greenwell Point	+45min	Swansea	-3min
Harrington	+1 min	Taree	+2hrs
Harrington Inlet	+16min	Tea Gardens	+1hr
Hexham	+1hr 10min	Terranora Inlet	+2hrs 10min
Huskisson	+3min	The Spit Bridge	0
Iluka	0	Trial Bay	0
Jervis Bay	-3min	Tweed Heads	+4min
Kempsey	+3hrs 15min	Ulladulla Harbour	0
Kendall	+3hrs 30min	Ulmarra	+4hrs 30min
Kiama	0	Wardell	+1 hr 30 min
Kurnell	0	Watson Taylors Lake	+2hrs
Lismore	+1hr 15min	Wauchope	+1hr 30min
Liverpool+	+2hrs 30min	Windsor	+5hrs 50min
Lower Portland Ferry	+3hrs 5min	Wingham	+3hrs 15min
Lugarno	+1hr	Wisemans Ferry	+2hrs 15min
Maclean	+2hrs 15min	Wollomba River mouth	+1hr 50min
Merimbula Lake Bridge	+1hr 30min	Wollongong	0
Milperra	+2hrs 10min	Wooli	+1hr 5min

Fort Denison

Day	Date		Tide 1	
Sun	1	●	2:20 AM	(0.54) L
Mon	2		2:57 AM	(0.56) L
Tue	3		3:36 AM	(0.57) L
Wed	4		4:17 AM	(0.59) L
THu	5		5:03 AM	(0.61) L
Fri	6		12:30 AM	(1.26) H
Sat	7		1:25 AM	(1.27) H
Sun	8		2:24 AM	(1.30) H
Mon	9		3:25 AM	(1.37) H
Tue	10		4:24 AM	(1.48) H
Wed	11		5:19 AM	(1.60) H
THu	12		6:13 AM	(1.72) H
Fri	13		12:31 AM	(0.42) L
Sat	14		1:21 AM	(0.44) L
Sun	15	○	2:10 AM	(0.46) L
Mon	16		2:59 AM	(0.48) L
Tue	17		3:47 AM	(0.52) L
Wed	18		4:35 AM	(0.55) L
THu	19		5:23 AM	(0.60) L
Fri	20		12:45 AM	(1.27) H
Sat	21		1:32 AM	(1.26) H
Sun	22		2:21 AM	(1.28) H
Mon	23		3:13 AM	(1.31) H
Tue	24		4:06 AM	(1.36) H
Wed	25		4:58 AM	(1.43) H
THu	26		5:45 AM	(1.50) H
Fri	27		6:30 AM	(1.58) H
Sat	28		12:32 AM	(0.61) L
Sun	29		1:15 AM	(0.60) L
Mon	30	●	1:57 AM	(0.58) L
Tue	31	●	2:39 AM	(0.55) L

Tide 2		Tide 3		Tide 4	
8:56 AM	(1.78) **H**	3:38 PM	(0.40) L	9:29 PM	(1.31) **H**
9:33 AM	(1.81) **H**	4:17 PM	(0.38) L	10:10 PM	(1.30) **H**
10:13 AM	(1.82) **H**	5:00 PM	(0.38) L	10:54 PM	(1.28) **H**
10:55 AM	(1.81) **H**	5:44 PM	(0.39) L	11:40 PM	(1.27) **H**
11:39 AM	(1.79) **H**	6:31 PM	(0.40) L		
5:54 AM	(0.64) L	12:27 PM	(1.75) **H**	7:22 PM	(0.42) L
6:50 AM	(0.66) L	1:18 PM	(1.70) **H**	8:15 PM	(0.42) L
7:54 AM	(0.68) L	2:15 PM	(1.63) **H**	9:09 PM	(0.42) L
9:04 AM	(0.67) L	3:20 PM	(1.57) **H**	10:01 PM	(0.41) L
10:19 AM	(0.63) L	4:28 PM	(1.51) **H**	10:52 PM	(0.41) L
11:33 AM	(0.56) L	5:33 PM	(1.46) **H**	11:43 PM	(0.41) L
12:42 PM	(0.46) L	6:37 PM	(1.43) **H**		
7:04 AM	(1.84) **H**	1:45 PM	(0.36) L	7:38 PM	(1.40) **H**
7:55 AM	(1.93) **H**	2:42 PM	(0.28) L	8:35 PM	(1.38) **H**
8:45 AM	(1.98) **H**	3:34 PM	(0.24) L	9:30 PM	(1.35) **H**
9:35 AM	(1.99) **H**	4:24 PM	(0.24) L	10:21 PM	(1.33) **H**
10:23 AM	(1.96) **H**	5:13 PM	(0.28) L	11:11 PM	(1.31) **H**
11:09 AM	(1.89) **H**	5:59 PM	(0.34) L	11:58 PM	(1.29) **H**
11:53 AM	(1.80) **H**	6:43 PM	(0.41) L		
6:11 AM	(0.65) L	12:36 PM	(1.69) **H**	7:26 PM	(0.48) L
7:00 AM	(0.71) L	1:18 PM	(1.57) **H**	8:07 PM	(0.53) L
7:55 AM	(0.76) L	2:03 PM	(1.46) **H**	8:49 PM	(0.57) L
8:57 AM	(0.79) L	2:55 PM	(1.36) **H**	9:32 PM	(0.59) L
10:06 AM	(0.79) L	3:54 PM	(1.28) **H**	10:17 PM	(0.61) L
11:17 AM	(0.76) L	4:58 PM	(1.24) **H**	11:03 PM	(0.61) L
12:22 PM	(0.69) L	6:00 PM	(1.22) **H**	11:48 PM	(0.62) L
1:16 PM	(0.61) L	6:56 PM	(1.22) **H**		
7:14 AM	(1.66) **H**	2:02 PM	(0.53) L	7:45 PM	(1.24) **H**
7:55 AM	(1.73) **H**	2:44 PM	(0.45) L	8:30 PM	(1.27) **H**
8:35 AM	(1.80) **H**	3:24 PM	(0.39) L	9:13 PM	(1.29) **H**
9:16 AM	(1.85) **H**	4:03 PM	(0.34) L	9:55 PM	(1.31) **H**

SOLAR/LUNAR

BITE TIMES

Apogee moon phase on Tuesday 24th
Perigee moon phase on Thursday 12th
● **New moon on Sunday 1st and Tuesday 31st**
First quarter moon on Monday 9th
○ **Full moon on Sunday 15th**
Last quarter moon phase on Monday 23rd

Sydney, NSW: Rise: 05:30am Set: 08:00pm
(Note: These sun rise/set times are averages for the month)

DAY	MINOR BITE	MAJOR BITE	MINOR BITE	MAJOR BITE	SALT WATER RATING	FRESH WATER RATING
SUN 1	3:17 AM	10:57 AM	6:44 PM	11:23 PM	● 8	8
MON 2	3:59 AM	11:50 AM	7:46 PM		8	6
TUE 3	4:50 AM	12:46 PM	8:42 PM	12:18 AM	7	6
WED 4	5:49 AM	1:43 PM	9:31 PM	1:14 AM	6	7
THUR 5	6:55 AM	2:38 PM	10:11 PM	2:10 AM	5	5
FRI 6	8:05 AM	3:31 PM	10:46 PM	3:04 AM	4	6
SAT 7	9:15 AM	4:21 PM	11:15 PM	3:55 AM	3	5
SUN 8	10:25 AM	5:09 PM	11:42 PM	4:45 AM	3	5
MON 9	11:35 AM	5:57 PM		5:32 AM	4	6
TUE 10	12:45 PM	6:44 PM	12:07 AM	6:20 AM	5	6
WED 11	1:57 PM	7:34 PM	12:33 AM	7:09 AM	3	5

DECEMBER 2024

DAY	MINOR BITE	MAJOR BITE	MINOR BITE	MAJOR BITE	SALT WATER RATING	FRESH WATER RATING
THUR 12	3:12 PM	8:27 PM	1:01 AM	8:00 AM	6	6
FRI 13	4:29 PM	9:24 PM	1:34 AM	8:55 AM	5	7
SAT 14	5:45 PM	10:25 PM	2:13 AM	9:54 AM	3	8
SUN 15	6:56 PM	11:28 PM	3:01 AM	10:56 AM	◯ 5	7
MON 16	7:58 PM		3:59 AM	11:58 AM	7	6
TUE 17	8:48 PM	12:30 AM	5:05 AM	12:59 PM	7	6
WED 18	9:28 PM	1:29 AM	6:14 AM	1:55 PM	5	5
THUR 19	10:00 PM	2:22 AM	7:23 AM	2:46 PM	5	5
FRI 20	10:26 PM	3:11 AM	8:29 AM	3:33 PM	4	4
SAT 21	10:49 PM	3:55 AM	9:32 AM	4:15 PM	3	6
SUN 22	11:10 PM	4:36 AM	10:31 AM	4:55 PM	4	4
MON 23	11:31 PM	5:15 AM	11:29 AM	5:34 PM	5	5
TUE 24	11:52 PM	5:54 AM	12:27 PM	6:14 PM	6	6
WED 25		6:34 AM	1:25 PM	6:54 PM	7	7
THUR 26	12:15 AM	7:15 AM	2:26 PM	7:37 PM	7	8
FRI 27	12:42 AM	8:00 AM	3:28 PM	8:24 PM	5	8
SAT 28	1:14 AM	8:49 AM	4:32 PM	9:15 PM	6	7
SUN 29	1:53 AM	9:41 AM	5:35 PM	10:08 PM	6	7
MON 30	2:41 AM	10:37 AM	6:34 PM	11:05 PM	8	8
TUE 31	3:38 AM	11:34 AM	7:26 PM		● 8	8

TIDE TIMES
Tim Smith's

POPULAR TIDE ADJUSTMENTS

Ballina Boat Dock	+15min	Morpeth	+3hrs 10min
Batemans Bay	-1min	Moruya	+30min
Bermagui	+5min	Murwillumbah	+2hrs 30min
Blackmans Point	+1hr 15min	Narooma	+40min
Botany Bay	+3min	Nelson Bay	+30min
Broughton Island	-6min	Peats Ferry Bridge	+1hr
Byron Bay	0	Pindimar	+45min
Chinderah	+1hr 15min	Pittwater Entrance	0
Clyde River Bridge	+15min	Port Hacking	+2min
Coffs Harbour	-2min	Port Hacking Audley	+ 30min
Como	+30min	Port Hacking Burraneer	+15min
Coraki	+4hrs	Port Hacking Lilli Pilli	+30min
Crookhaven Jetty	+15min	Port Macquarie	+21min
Crowdy Head	0	Port Stephens	0
Danger Island	+18min	Queens Lake	+2hrs
Dolls Point	+15min	Raleigh	+1hr
Ettalong	+30min	Raymond Terrace	+1hr 55min
Evans Head Bridge	0	Salamander Bay	+45min
Fig Tree Bridge	+15min	Sandon	+30min
Forster	+1min	Shoalhaven Riv' Nowra	+2hrs 10min
Gabo Island	-9min	Shoalhaven Riv'O'Keefes Pt	+2hrs
Gladesville Bridge	+15min	Silverwater Bridge	+15min
Gladstone	+2hrs 10min	Soldiers Point	+1hr
Grafton	+4hrs 1 min	South West Rocks	+1hr 2min
Greenwell Point	+45min	Swansea	-3min
Harrington	+1 min	Taree	+2hrs
Harrington Inlet	+16min	Tea Gardens	+1hr
Hexham	+1hr 10min	Terranora Inlet	+2hrs 10min
Huskisson	+3min	The Spit Bridge	0
Iluka	0	Trial Bay	0
Jervis Bay	-3min	Tweed Heads	+4min
Kempsey	+3hrs 15min	Ulladulla Harbour	0
Kendall	+3hrs 30min	Ulmarra	+4hrs 30min
Kiama	0	Wardell	+1 hr 30 min
Kurnell	0	Watson Taylors Lake	+1hr
Lismore	+1hr 15min	Wauchope	+1hr 30min
Liverpool+	+2hrs 30min	Windsor	+5hrs 50min
Lower Portland Ferry	+3hrs 5min	Wingham	+3hrs 15min
Lugarno	+1hr	Wisemans Ferry	+2hrs 15min
Maclean	+2hrs 15min	Wollomba River mouth	+1hr 50min
Merimbula Lake Bridge	+1hr 30min	Wollongong	0
Milperra	+2hrs 10min	Wooli	+1hr 5min

Fort Denison

Day	Date	Tide 1	
Wed	1	3:22 AM	(0.54) L
THu	2	4:07 AM	(0.52) L
Fri	3	4:54 AM	(0.52) L
Sat	4	12:11 AM	(1.38) H
Sun	5	1:01 AM	(1.41) H
Mon	6	1:55 AM	(1.45) H
Tue	7	2:51 AM	(1.50) H
Wed	8	3:50 AM	(1.57) H
THu	9	4:51 AM	(1.65) H
Fri	10	5:51 AM	(1.73) H
Sat	11	12:09 AM	(0.55) L
Sun	12	1:06 AM	(0.55) L
Mon	13	2:00 AM	(0.53) L
Tue	14 ○	2:49 AM	(0.51) L
Wed	15	3:35 AM	(0.51) L
THu	16	4:19 AM	(0.52) L
Fri	17	5:01 AM	(0.55) L
Sat	18	12:06 AM	(1.36) H
Sun	19	12:45 AM	(1.36) H
Mon	20	1:26 AM	(1.37) H
Tue	21	2:10 AM	(1.39) H
Wed	22	3:00 AM	(1.41) H
THu	23	3:57 AM	(1.43) H
Fri	24	4:55 AM	(1.48) H
Sat	25	5:52 AM	(1.54) H
Sun	26	12:00 AM	(0.69) L
Mon	27	12:51 AM	(0.64) L
Tue	28	1:39 AM	(0.58) L
Wed	29 ●	2:24 AM	(0.51) L
THu	30	3:10 AM	(0.45) L
Fri	31	3:56 AM	(0.41) L

Tide 2		Tide 3		Tide 4	
9:59 AM	(1.90) H	4:45 PM	(0.32) L	10:39 PM	(1.34) H
10:42 AM	(1.91) H	5:27 PM	(0.31) L	11:24 PM	(1.36) H
11:26 AM	(1.89) H	6:10 PM	(0.31) L		
5:45 AM	(0.54) L	12:12 PM	(1.83) H	6:55 PM	(0.33) L
6:40 AM	(0.57) L	1:00 PM	(1.74) H	7:41 PM	(0.37) L
7:41 AM	(0.60) L	1:52 PM	(1.62) H	8:29 PM	(0.41) L
8:48 AM	(0.63) L	2:52 PM	(1.48) H	9:18 PM	(0.47) L
10:06 AM	(0.63) L	4:02 PM	(1.37) H	10:13 PM	(0.51) L
11:28 AM	(0.58) L	5:19 PM	(1.29) H	11:11 PM	(0.54) L
12:43 PM	(0.50) L	6:32 PM	(1.27) H		
6:50 AM	(1.81) H	1:46 PM	(0.41) L	7:37 PM	(1.28) H
7:45 AM	(1.88) H	2:40 PM	(0.34) L	8:32 PM	(1.31) H
8:36 AM	(1.92) H	3:28 PM	(0.30) L	9:21 PM	(1.33) H
9:24 AM	(1.93) H	4:11 PM	(0.29) L	10:05 PM	(1.35) H
10:08 AM	(1.91) H	4:51 PM	(0.32) L	10:47 PM	(1.36) H
10:48 AM	(1.86) H	5:28 PM	(0.36) L	11:27 PM	(1.36) H
11:26 AM	(1.77) H	6:02 PM	(0.41) L		
5:43 AM	(0.60) L	12:01 PM	(1.67) H	6:35 PM	(0.47) L
6:26 AM	(0.65) L	12:37 PM	(1.56) H	7:07 PM	(0.52) L
7:13 AM	(0.71) L	1:15 PM	(1.44) H	7:41 PM	(0.57) L
8:08 AM	(0.76) L	1:59 PM	(1.33) H	8:19 PM	(0.62) L
9:15 AM	(0.78) L	2:55 PM	(1.23) H	9:06 PM	(0.67) L
10:31 AM	(0.78) L	4:06 PM	(1.16) H	10:01 PM	(0.70) L
11:49 AM	(0.73) L	5:25 PM	(1.14) H	11:01 PM	(0.71) L
12:52 PM	(0.64) L	6:33 PM	(1.16) H		
6:44 AM	(1.62) H	1:42 PM	(0.55) L	7:28 PM	(1.21) H
7:31 AM	(1.72) H	2:25 PM	(0.46) L	8:13 PM	(1.27) H
8:16 AM	(1.81) H	3:04 PM	(0.37) L	8:55 PM	(1.33) H
9:00 AM	(1.90) H	3:44 PM	(0.30) L	9:36 PM	(1.39) H
9:43 AM	(1.95) H	4:22 PM	(0.25) L	10:18 PM	(1.45) H
10:26 AM	(1.97) H	5:02 PM	(0.22) L	11:02 PM	(1.50) H

SOLAR/LUNAR BITE TIMES

Tim Smith's

Apogee moon phase on Tuesday 21st
Perigee moon phase on Wednesday 8th
● **New moon on Wednesday 29th**
First quarter moon on Tuesday 7th
○ **Full moon on Tuesday 14th**
Last quarter moon phase on Wednesday 22nd

Sydney, NSW: Rise: 05:50am Set: 08:00pm
(Note: These sun rise/set times are averages for the month)

DAY	MINOR BITE	MAJOR BITE	MINOR BITE	MAJOR BITE	SALT WATER RATING	FRESH WATER RATING
WED 1	4:44 AM	12:31 PM	8:10 PM	12:02 AM	8	6
THUR 2	5:54 AM	1:26 PM	8:47 PM	12:58 AM	7	6
FRI 3	7:06 AM	2:18 PM	9:18 PM	1:52 AM	6	7
SAT 4	8:17 AM	3:07 PM	9:46 PM	2:42 AM	5	5
SUN 5	9:27 AM	3:55 PM	10:11 PM	3:30 AM	4	6
MON 6	10:37 AM	4:42 PM	10:36 PM	4:18 AM	3	5
TUE 7	11:47 AM	5:30 PM	11:03 PM	5:05 AM	4	6
WED 8	12:59 PM	6:20 PM	11:33 PM	5:55 AM	5	6
THUR 9	2:13 PM	7:14 PM		6:46 AM	4	5
FRI 10	3:27 PM	8:12 PM	12:08 AM	7:43 AM	3	5
SAT 11	4:39 PM	9:13 PM	12:52 AM	8:42 AM	6	6

POPULAR LOCATION ADJUSTMENTS (See full list on page 7)

DAY	MINOR BITE	MAJOR BITE	MINOR BITE	MAJOR BITE	SALT WATER RATING	FRESH WATER RATING
SUN 12	5:43 PM	10:14 PM	1:44 AM	9:43 AM	5	7
MON 13	6:38 PM	11:14 PM	2:46 AM	10:43 AM	3	8
TUE 14	7:22 PM		3:54 AM	11:41 AM ○	5	7
WED 15	7:57 PM	12:09 AM	5:03 AM	12:34 PM	7	6
THUR 16	8:26 PM	1:00 AM	6:11 AM	1:23 PM	7	6
FRI 17	8:50 PM	1:47 AM	7:16 AM	2:07 PM	5	5
SAT 18	9:12 PM	2:29 AM	8:18 AM	2:49 PM	4	4
SUN 19	9:33 PM	3:10 AM	9:17 AM	3:29 PM	3	6
MON 20	9:54 PM	3:49 AM	10:15 AM	4:08 PM	3	6
TUE 21	10:16 PM	4:29 AM	11:13 AM	4:48 PM	4	4
WED 22	10:41 PM	5:09 AM	12:13 PM	5:30 PM	5	5
THUR 23	11:10 PM	5:52 AM	1:14 PM	6:15 PM	6	6
FRI 24	11:46 PM	6:39 AM	2:17 PM	7:03 PM	7	7
SAT 25		7:29 AM	3:20 PM	7:56 PM	7	8
SUN 26	12:29 AM	8:23 AM	4:20 PM	8:51 PM	5	8
MON 27	1:23 AM	9:20 AM	5:15 PM	9:48 PM	6	7
TUE 28	2:26 AM	10:18 AM	6:03 PM	10:46 PM	8	8
WED 29	3:35 AM	11:15 AM	6:44 PM	11:41 PM ●	8	8
THUR 30	4:48 AM	12:09 PM	7:18 PM		8	6
FRI 31	6:02 AM	1:01 PM	7:47 PM	12:35 AM	7	6

TIDE TIMES

Tim Smith's

POPULAR TIDE ADJUSTMENTS

Ballina Boat Dock	+15min	Morpeth	+3hrs 10min
Batemans Bay	-1min	Moruya	+30min
Bermagui	+5min	Murwillumbah	+2hrs 30min
Blackmans Point	+1hr 15min	Narooma	+40min
Botany Bay	+3min	Nelson Bay	+30min
Broughton Island	-6min	Peats Ferry Bridge	+1hr
Byron Bay	0	Pindimar	+45min
Chinderah	+1hr 15min	Pittwater Entrance	0
Clyde River Bridge	+15min	Port Hacking	+2min
Coffs Harbour	-2min	Port Hacking Audley	+30min
Como	+30min	Port Hacking Burraneer	+15min
Coraki	+4hrs	Port Hacking Lilli Pilli	+30min
Crookhaven Jetty	+15min	Port Macquarie	+21min
Crowdy Head	0	Port Stephens	0
Danger Island	+18min	Queens Lake	+2hrs
Dolls Point	+15min	Raleigh	+1hr
Ettalong	+30min	Raymond Terrace	+1hr 55min
Evans Head Bridge	0	Salamander Bay	+45min
Fig Tree Bridge	+15min	Sandon	+30min
Forster	+1min	Shoalhaven Riv' Nowra	+2hrs 10min
Gabo Island	-9min	Shoalhaven Riv'O'Keefes Pt	+2hrs
Gladesville Bridge	+15min	Silverwater Bridge	+15min
Gladstone	+2hrs 10min	Soldiers Point	+1hr
Grafton	+4hrs 1 min	South West Rocks	+1hr 2min
Greenwell Point	+45min	Swansea	-3min
Harrington	+1 min	Taree	+2hrs
Harrington Inlet	+16min	Tea Gardens	+1hr
Hexham	+1hr 10min	Terranora Inlet	+2hrs 10min
Huskisson	+3min	The Spit Bridge	0
Iluka	0	Trial Bay	0
Jervis Bay	-3min	Tweed Heads	+4min
Kempsey	+3hrs 15min	Ulladulla Harbour	0
Kendall	+3hrs 30min	Ulmarra	+4hrs 30min
Kiama	0	Wardell	+1 hr 30 min
Kurnell	0	Watson Taylors Lake	+2hrs
Lismore	+1hr 15min	Wauchope	+1hr 30min
Liverpool+	+2hrs 30min	Windsor	+5hrs 50min
Lower Portland Ferry	+3hrs 5min	Wingham	+3hrs 15min
Lugarno	+1hr	Wisemans Ferry	+2hrs 15min
Maclean	+2hrs 15min	Wollomba River mouth	+1hr 50min
Merimbula Lake Bridge	+1hr 30min	Wollongong	0
Milperra	+2hrs 10min	Wooli	+1hr 5min

Fort Denison

Day	Date		Tide 1	
Sat	1	4:45 AM	(0.40)	L
Sun	2	5:36 AM	(0.42)	L
Mon	3	12:34 AM	(1.58)	H
Tue	4	1:25 AM	(1.60)	H
Wed	5	2:19 AM	(1.61)	H
THu	6	3:20 AM	(1.62)	H
Fri	7	4:29 AM	(1.64)	H
Sat	8	5:39 AM	(1.68)	H
Sun	9	12:02 AM	(0.65)	L
Mon	10	1:03 AM	(0.60)	L
Tue	11	1:55 AM	(0.55)	L
Wed	12	2:41 AM	(0.50)	L
THu	13 ○	3:23 AM	(0.48)	L
Fri	14	4:01 AM	(0.49)	L
Sat	15	4:39 AM	(0.51)	L
Sun	16	5:17 AM	(0.54)	L
Mon	17	12:00 AM	(1.49)	H
Tue	18	12:35 AM	(1.49)	H
Wed	19	1:14 AM	(1.48)	H
THu	20	1:59 AM	(1.47)	H
Fri	21	2:54 AM	(1.45)	H
Sat	22	4:01 AM	(1.46)	H
Sun	23	5:12 AM	(1.51)	H
Mon	24	6:13 AM	(1.59)	H
Tue	25	12:30 AM	(0.67)	L
Wed	26	1:21 AM	(0.57)	L
THu	27	2:08 AM	(0.47)	L
Fri	28 ●	2:55 AM	(0.38)	L

FEBRUARY 2025

Tide 2		Tide 3		Tide 4	
11:10 AM	(1.93) H	5:43 PM	(0.24) L	11:47 PM	(1.55) H
11:55 AM	(1.83) H	6:23 PM	(0.29) L		
6:30 AM	(0.46) L	12:43 PM	(1.69) H	7:05 PM	(0.37) L
7:31 AM	(0.52) L	1:35 PM	(1.52) H	7:50 PM	(0.46) L
8:41 AM	(0.58) L	2:36 PM	(1.35) H	8:41 PM	(0.56) L
10:02 AM	(0.61) L	3:52 PM	(1.22) H	9:42 PM	(0.63) L
11:29 AM	(0.58) L	5:21 PM	(1.17) H	10:52 PM	(0.67) L
12:45 PM	(0.52) L	6:40 PM	(1.20) H		
6:43 AM	(1.74) H	1:44 PM	(0.44) L	7:38 PM	(1.26) H
7:39 AM	(1.80) H	2:30 PM	(0.38) L	8:26 PM	(1.32) H
8:27 AM	(1.83) H	3:12 PM	(0.35) L	9:06 PM	(1.37) H
9:10 AM	(1.84) H	3:47 PM	(0.34) L	9:44 PM	(1.41) H
9:48 AM	(1.82) H	4:20 PM	(0.35) L	10:19 PM	(1.44) H
10:23 AM	(1.77) H	4:50 PM	(0.38) L	10:53 PM	(1.46) H
10:57 AM	(1.70) H	5:18 PM	(0.42) L	11:26 PM	(1.48) H
11:30 AM	(1.61) H	5:45 PM	(0.47) L		
5:58 AM	(0.59) L	12:02 PM	(1.51) H	6:13 PM	(0.52) L
6:41 AM	(0.64) L	12:38 PM	(1.40) H	6:43 PM	(0.59) L
7:31 AM	(0.70) L	1:20 PM	(1.29) H	7:17 PM	(0.65) L
8:31 AM	(0.74) L	2:13 PM	(1.19) H	8:01 PM	(0.72) L
9:46 AM	(0.76) L	3:23 PM	(1.12) H	9:01 PM	(0.78) L
11:11 AM	(0.73) L	4:52 PM	(1.10) H	10:17 PM	(0.79) L
12:20 PM	(0.65) L	6:10 PM	(1.15) H	11:30 PM	(0.75) L
1:13 PM	(0.55) L	7:05 PM	(1.23) H		
7:05 AM	(1.71) H	1:56 PM	(0.44) L	7:49 PM	(1.32) H
7:51 AM	(1.82) H	2:35 PM	(0.34) L	8:30 PM	(1.42) H
8:36 AM	(1.91) H	3:14 PM	(0.25) L	9:12 PM	(1.52) H
9:20 AM	(1.96) H	3:52 PM	(0.21) L	9:53 PM	(1.62) H

SOLAR/LUNAR BITE TIMES

Tim Smith's

Apogee moon phase on Tuesday 18th
Perigee moon phase on Sunday 2nd
● **New moon on Friday 28th**
First quarter moon on Wednesday 5th
○ **Full moon on Thursday 13th**
Last quarter moon phase on Friday 21st

Sydney, NSW: Rise: 06:20am Set: 07:40pm
(Note: These sun rise/set times are averages for the month)

DAY	MINOR BITE	MAJOR BITE	MINOR BITE	MAJOR BITE	SALT WATER RATING	FRESH WATER RATING
SAT 1	7:15 AM	1:50 PM	8:14 PM	1:25 AM	6	7
SUN 2	8:26 AM	2:39 PM	8:40 PM	2:14 AM	5	5
MON 3	9:38 AM	3:27 PM	9:06 PM	3:02 AM	4	6
TUE 4	10:50 AM	4:17 PM	9:35 PM	3:52 AM	3	5
WED 5	12:04 PM	5:10 PM	10:09 PM	4:43 AM	4	6
THUR 6	1:18 PM	6:06 PM	10:49 PM	5:38 AM	5	6
FRI 7	2:29 PM	7:05 PM	11:37 PM	6:35 AM	4	5
SAT 8	3:35 PM	8:05 PM		7:34 AM	3	5
SUN 9	4:32 PM	9:04 PM	12:35 AM	8:34 AM	6	6
MON 10	5:18 PM	10:00 PM	1:40 AM	9:31 AM	5	7

DAY	MINOR BITE	MAJOR BITE	MINOR BITE	MAJOR BITE	SALT WATER RATING	FRESH WATER RATING
UE 11	5:56 PM	10:52 PM	2:48 AM	10:26 AM	3	8
WED 12	6:26 PM	11:40 PM	3:56 AM	11:16 AM	5	7
THUR 13	6:52 PM		5:01 AM	12:01 PM	◯ 5	7
RI 14	7:15 PM	12:24 AM	6:04 AM	12:44 PM	7	6
SAT 15	7:36 PM	1:05 AM	7:05 AM	1:24 PM	7	6
SUN 16	7:57 PM	1:45 AM	8:04 AM	2:04 PM	5	5
MON 17	8:18 PM	2:24 AM	9:02 AM	2:43 PM	4	4
TUE 18	8:42 PM	3:04 AM	10:01 AM	3:24 PM	3	6
WED 19	9:09 PM	3:46 AM	11:01 AM	4:08 PM	4	4
THUR 20	9:41 PM	4:31 AM	12:03 PM	4:55 PM	4	4
RI 21	10:20 PM	5:19 AM	1:05 PM	5:45 PM	5	5
SAT 22	11:08 PM	6:11 AM	2:06 PM	6:37 PM	6	6
SUN 23		7:05 AM	3:03 PM	7:33 PM	7	7
MON 24	12:06 AM	8:02 AM	3:53 PM	8:30 PM	7	8
TUE 25	1:12 AM	8:59 AM	4:37 PM	9:26 PM	5	8
WED 26	2:23 AM	9:54 AM	5:14 PM	10:21 PM	6	7
THUR 27	3:38 AM	10:48 AM	5:45 PM	11:13 PM	8	8
RI 28	4:52 AM	11:39 AM	6:14 PM		● 8	8

TIDE TIMES

Tim Smith's

POPULAR TIDE ADJUSTMENTS

Ballina Boat Dock	+15min	Morpeth	+3hrs 10min
Batemans Bay	-1min	Moruya	+30min
Bermagui	+5min	Murwillumbah	+2hrs 30min
Blackmans Point	+1hr 15min	Narooma	+40min
Botany Bay	+3min	Nelson Bay	+30min
Broughton Island	-6min	Peats Ferry Bridge	+1hr
Byron Bay	0	Pindimar	+45min
Chinderah	+1hr 15min	Pittwater Entrance	0
Clyde River Bridge	+4hrs	Port Hacking	+2min
Coffs Harbour	-2min	Port Hacking Audley	+ 30min
Como	+30min	Port Hacking Burraneer	+15min
Coraki	+4hrs	Port Hacking Lilli Pilli	+30min
Crookhaven Jetty	+15min	Port Macquarie	+21min
Crowdy Head	0	Port Stephens	0
Danger Island	+18min	Queens Lake	+2hrs
Dolls Point	+15min	Raleigh	+1hr
Ettalong	+30min	Raymond Terrace	+1hr 55min
Evans Head Bridge	0	Salamander Bay	+45min
Fig Tree Bridge	+15min	Sandon	+30min
Forster	+1min	Shoalhaven Riv' Nowra	+2hrs 10min
Gabo Island	-9min	Shoalhaven Riv'O'Keefes Pt	+2hrs
Gladesville Bridge	+15min	Silverwater Bridge	+15min
Gladstone	+2hrs 10min	Soldiers Point	+1hr
Grafton	+4hrs 1 min	South West Rocks	+1hr 2min
Greenwell Point	+45min	Swansea	-3min
Harrington	+1 min	Taree	+2hrs
Harrington Inlet	+16min	Tea Gardens	+1hr
Hexham	+1hr 10min	Terranora Inlet	+2hrs 10min
Huskisson	+3min	The Spit Bridge	0
Iluka	0	Trial Bay	0
Jervis Bay	-3min	Tweed Heads	+4min
Kempsey	+3hrs 15min	Ulladulla Harbour	0
Kendall	+3hrs 30min	Ulmarra	+4hrs 30min
Kiama	0	Wardell	+1 hr 30 min
Kurnell	0	Watson Taylors Lake	+2hrs
Lismore	+1hr 15min	Wauchope	+1hr 30min
Liverpool+	+2hrs 30min	Windsor	+5hrs 50min
Lower Portland Ferry	+3hrs 5min	Wingham	+3hrs 15min
Lugarno	+1hr	Wisemans Ferry	+2hrs 15min
Maclean	+2hrs 15min	Wollomba River mouth	+1hr 50min
Merimbula Lake Bridge	+1hr 30min	Wollongong	0
Milperra	+2hrs 10min	Wooli	+1hr 5min

Fort Denison

Day	Date	Tide 1	
Sat	1	3:44 AM	(0.33) L
Sun	2	4:34 AM	(0.31) L
Mon	3	5:28 AM	(0.33) L
Tue	4	12:08 AM	(1.77) H
Wed	5	12:58 AM	(1.76) H
THu	6	1:52 AM	(1.71) H
Fri	7	2:58 AM	(1.66) H
Sat	8	4:13 AM	(1.63) H
Sun	9	5:29 AM	(1.64) H
Mon	10	12:00 AM	(0.71) L
Tue	11	12:59 AM	(0.64) L
Wed	12	1:46 AM	(0.57) L
THu	13	2:29 AM	(0.52) L
Fri	14 ○	3:07 AM	(0.50) L
Sat	15	3:43 AM	(0.49) L
Sun	16	4:19 AM	(0.50) L
Mon	17	4:57 AM	(0.52) L
Tue	18	5:35 AM	(0.56) L
Wed	19	6:17 AM	(0.60) L
THu	20	12:29 AM	(1.59) H
Fri	21	1:11 AM	(1.55) H
Sat	22	2:04 AM	(1.51) H
Sun	23	3:13 AM	(1.49) H
Mon	24	4:29 AM	(1.52) H
Tue	25	5:36 AM	(1.61) H
Wed	26	12:03 AM	(0.68) L
THu	27	12:59 AM	(0.56) L
Fri	28	1:49 AM	(0.45) L
Sat	29 ●	2:40 AM	(0.35) L
Sun	30	3:31 AM	(0.29) L
Mon	31	4:25 AM	(0.27) L

Tide 2		Tide 3		Tide 4	
10:05 AM	(1.94) **H**	4:30 PM	(0.20) L	10:36 PM	(1.70) **H**
10:52 AM	(1.87) **H**	5:10 PM	(0.25) L	11:21 PM	(1.75) **H**
11:40 AM	(1.74) **H**	5:50 PM	(0.33) L		
6:25 AM	(0.39) L	12:30 PM	(1.57) **H**	6:31 PM	(0.44) L
7:27 AM	(0.46) L	1:26 PM	(1.40) **H**	7:17 PM	(0.56) L
8:39 AM	(0.54) L	2:32 PM	(1.25) **H**	8:13 PM	(0.67) L
10:02 AM	(0.58) L	3:58 PM	(1.16) **H**	9:24 PM	(0.75) L
11:26 AM	(0.57) L	5:30 PM	(1.17) **H**	10:46 PM	(0.76) L
12:34 PM	(0.53) L	6:38 PM	(1.23) **H**		
6:32 AM	(1.68) **H**	1:27 PM	(0.48) L	7:27 PM	(1.31) **H**
7:25 AM	(1.72) **H**	2:08 PM	(0.44) L	8:07 PM	(1.39) **H**
8:08 AM	(1.74) **H**	2:43 PM	(0.42) L	8:43 PM	(1.45) **H**
8:46 AM	(1.73) **H**	3:14 PM	(0.41) L	9:16 PM	(1.51) **H**
9:21 AM	(1.71) **H**	3:42 PM	(0.42) L	9:47 PM	(1.55) **H**
9:54 AM	(1.66) **H**	4:08 PM	(0.44) L	10:18 PM	(1.59) **H**
10:27 AM	(1.60) **H**	4:32 PM	(0.48) L	10:48 PM	(1.61) **H**
11:00 AM	(1.52) **H**	4:59 PM	(0.52) L	11:19 PM	(1.63) **H**
11:35 AM	(1.44) **H**	5:25 PM	(0.58) L	11:52 PM	(1.62) **H**
12:13 PM	(1.35) **H**	5:55 PM	(0.65) L		
7:04 AM	(0.65) L	12:55 PM	(1.26) **H**	6:30 PM	(0.71) L
8:00 AM	(0.70) L	1:46 PM	(1.18) **H**	7:14 PM	(0.78) l
9:11 AM	(0.73) L	2:55 PM	(1.13) **H**	8:16 PM	(0.83) L
10:30 AM	(0.71) L	4:22 PM	(1.13) **H**	9:39 PM	(0.84) L
11:38 AM	(0.64) L	5:38 PM	(1.20) **H**	11:00 PM	(0.79) L
12:31 PM	(0.53) L	6:33 PM	(1.30) **H**		
6:31 AM	(1.72) **H**	1:15 PM	(0.43) L	7:18 PM	(1.43) **H**
7:21 AM	(1.82) **H**	1:56 PM	(0.33) L	8:00 PM	(1.56) **H**
8:08 AM	(1.88) **H**	2:35 PM	(0.27) L	8:43 PM	(1.70) **H**
8:56 AM	(1.89) **H**	3:15 PM	(0.25) L	9:25 PM	(1.81) **H**
9:44 AM	(1.84) **H**	3:55 PM	(0.27) L	10:10 PM	(1.90) **H**
10:34 AM	(1.74) **H**	4:36 PM	(0.34) L	10:55 PM	(1.94) **H**

SOLAR/LUNAR BITE TIMES

Apogee moon phase on Tuesday 18th

Perigee moon phase on Sunday 2nd and Sunday 30th

● **New moon on Saturday 29th**

First quarter moon on Friday 7th

○ **Full moon on Friday 14th**

Last quarter moon phase on Saturday 22nd

Sydney, NSW: Rise: 06:50am Set: 07:10pm

(Note: These sun rise/set times are averages for the month)

DAY	MINOR BITE	MAJOR BITE	MINOR BITE	MAJOR BITE	SALT WATER RATING	FRESH WATER RATING
SAT 1	6:06 AM	12:29 PM	6:41 PM	12:04 AM	8	6
SUN 2	7:20 AM	1:19 PM	7:07 PM	12:54 AM	7	6
MON 3	8:35 AM	2:10 PM	7:36 PM	1:44 AM	6	7
TUE 4	9:51 AM	3:04 PM	8:09 PM	2:37 AM	5	5
WED 5	11:07 AM	4:00 PM	8:47 PM	3:31 AM	4	6
THUR 6	12:21 PM	4:59 PM	9:34 PM	4:29 AM	3	5
FRI 7	1:29 PM	6:00 PM	10:29 PM	5:29 AM	4	6
SAT 8	2:29 PM	6:59 PM	11:31 PM	6:29 AM	5	6
SUN 9	3:18 PM	7:56 PM		7:27 AM	4	5
MON 10	3:57 PM	8:48 PM	12:38 AM	8:22 AM	3	5
TUE 11	4:29 PM	9:36 PM	1:45 AM	9:11 AM	6	6

MARCH 2025

POPULAR LOCATION ADJUSTMENTS (See full list on page 7)

DAY	MINOR BITE	MAJOR BITE	MINOR BITE	MAJOR BITE	SALT WATER RATING	FRESH WATER RATING
ED 12	4:56 PM	10:21 PM	2:51 AM	9:58 AM	5	7
UR 13	5:19 PM	11:02 PM	3:54 AM	10:41 AM	3	8
14	5:40 PM	11:42 PM	4:55 AM	11:22 AM	○ 5	7
T 15	6:01 PM		5:54 AM	12:01 PM	7	6
N 16	6:22 PM	12:22 AM	6:52 AM	12:41 PM	7	6
ON 17	6:45 PM	1:02 AM	7:51 AM	1:22 PM	7	6
E 18	7:10 PM	1:43 AM	8:51 AM	2:04 PM	5	5
ED 19	7:40 PM	2:26 AM	9:52 AM	2:49 PM	4	4
UR 20	8:16 PM	3:13 AM	10:54 AM	3:37 PM	3	6
I 21	9:00 PM	4:02 AM	11:54 AM	4:28 PM	4	4
T 22	9:52 PM	4:55 AM	12:52 PM	5:22 PM	5	5
N 23	10:53 PM	5:49 AM	1:44 PM	6:17 PM	6	6
ON 24		6:45 AM	2:29 PM	7:11 PM	7	7
E 25	12:00 AM	7:39 AM	3:08 PM	8:06 PM	7	8
ED 26	1:12 AM	8:33 AM	3:41 PM	8:58 PM	5	8
UR 27	2:25 AM	9:24 AM	4:11 PM	9:49 PM	6	7
I 28	3:39 AM	10:15 AM	4:38 PM	10:40 PM	8	8
T 29	4:53 AM	11:05 AM	5:05 PM	11:30 PM	● 8	8
N 30	6:09 AM	11:57 AM	5:33 PM		8	6
ON 31	7:27 AM	12:51 PM	6:05 PM	12:24 AM	7	6

TIDE TIMES

Tim Smith's

POPULAR TIDE ADJUSTMENTS

Ballina Boat Dock	+15min	Morpeth	+3hrs 10min
Batemans Bay	-1min	Moruya	+30min
Bermagui	+5min	Murwillumbah	+2hrs 30min
Blackmans Point	+1hr 15min	Narooma	+40min
Botany Bay	+3min	Nelson Bay	+30min
Broughton Island	-6min	Peats Ferry Bridge	+1hr
Byron Bay	0	Pindimar	+45min
Chinderah	+1hr 15min	Pittwater Entrance	0
Clyde River Bridge	+15min	Port Hacking	+2min
Coffs Harbour	-2min	Port Hacking Audley	+ 30min
Como	+30min	Port Hacking Burraneer	+15min
Coraki	+4hrs	Port Hacking Lilli Pilli	+30min
Crookhaven Jetty	+15min	Port Macquarie	+21min
Crowdy Head	0	Port Stephens	0
Danger Island	+18min	Queens Lake	+2hrs
Dolls Point	+15min	Raleigh	+1hr
Ettalong	+30min	Raymond Terrace	+1hr 55min
Evans Head Bridge	0	Salamander Bay	+45min
Fig Tree Bridge	+15min	Sandon	+30min
Forster	+1min	Shoalhaven Riv' Nowra	+2hrs 10min
Gabo Island	-9min	Shoalhaven Riv'O'Keefes Pt	+2hrs
Gladesville Bridge	+15min	Silverwater Bridge	+15min
Gladstone	+2hrs 10min	Soldiers Point	+1hr
Grafton	+4hrs 1 min	South West Rocks	+1hr 2min
Greenwell Point	+45min	Swansea	-3min
Harrington	+1 min	Taree	+2hrs
Harrington Inlet	+16min	Tea Gardens	+1hr
Hexham	+1hr 10min	Terranora Inlet	+2hrs 10min
Huskisson	+3min	The Spit Bridge	0
Iluka	0	Trial Bay	0
Jervis Bay	-3min	Tweed Heads	+4min
Kempsey	+3hrs 15min	Ulladulla Harbour	0
Kendall	+3hrs 30min	Ulmarra	+4hrs 30min
Kiama	0	Wardell	+1 hr 30 min
Kurnell	0	Watson Taylors Lake	+2hrs
Lismore	+1hr 15min	Wauchope	+1hr 30min
Liverpool+	+2hrs 30min	Windsor	+5hrs 50min
Lower Portland Ferry	+3hrs 5min	Wingham	+3hrs 15min
Lugarno	+1hr	Wisemans Ferry	+2hrs 15min
Maclean	+2hrs 15min	Wollomba River mouth	+1hr 50min
Merimbula Lake Bridge	+1hr 30min	Wollongong	0
Milperra	+2hrs 10min	Wooli	+1hr 5min

Fort Denison

Day	Date		Tide 1	
Tue	1		5:21 AM	(0.29) L
Wed	2		6:19 AM	(0.35) L
THu	3		12:34 AM	(1.88)
Fri	4		1:31 AM	(1.79)
Sat	5		2:38 AM	(1.70)
Sun	6		2:55 AM	(1.63)
Mon	7		4:08 AM	(1.61) H
Tue	8		5:08 AM	(1.62) H
Wed	9		5:57 AM	(1.63) H
THu	10		12:30 AM	(0.63) L
Fri	11		1:10 AM	(0.58) L
Sat	12		1:48 AM	(0.55) L
Sun	13	○	2:25 AM	(0.53) L
Mon	14		3:00 AM	(0.52) L
Tue	15		3:38 AM	(0.52) L
Wed	16		4:17 AM	(0.55) L
THu	17		5:00 AM	(0.58) L
Fri	18		5:45 AM	(0.63) L
Sat	19		6:40 AM	(0.67) L
Sun	20		12:32 AM	(1.60) H
Mon	21		1:36 AM	(1.58) H
Tue	22		2:48 AM	(1.59) H
Wed	23		3:56 AM	(1.65) H
THu	24		4:54 AM	(1.71) H
Fri	25		5:47 AM	(1.76) H
Sat	26		12:31 AM	(0.46) L
Sun	27		1:26 AM	(0.36) L
Mon	28	●	2:21 AM	(0.29) L
Tue	29		3:16 AM	(0.27) L
Wed	30		4:14 AM	(0.29) L

Tide 2		Tide 3		Tide 4	
11:27 AM	(1.60) H	5:18 PM	(0.44) L	11:44 PM	(1.93) H
12:22 PM	(1.45) H	6:03 PM	(0.56) L		
7:24 AM	(0.44) L	1:23 PM	(1.32) H	6:54 PM	(0.67) L
8:36 AM	(0.51) L	2:34 PM	(1.22) H	7:56 PM	(0.77) L
9:54 AM	(0.57) L	3:59 PM	(1.20) H	9:13 PM	(0.82) L
10:05 AM	(0.58) L	4:16 PM	(1.23) H	9:34 PM	(0.81) L
11:04 AM	(0.57) L	5:15 PM	(1.31) H	10:45 PM	(0.76) L
11:51 AM	(0.54) L	6:00 PM	(1.39) H	11:43 PM	(0.69) L
12:28 PM	(0.52) L	6:38 PM	(1.47) H		
6:37 AM	(1.62) H	1:00 PM	(0.51) L	7:12 PM	(1.55) H
7:15 AM	(1.61) H	1:29 PM	(0.50) L	7:44 PM	(1.61) H
7:49 AM	(1.58) H	1:56 PM	(0.51) L	8:14 PM	(1.67) H
8:24 AM	(1.54) H	2:22 PM	(0.53) L	8:43 PM	(1.71) H
8:59 AM	(1.49) H	2:48 PM	(0.56) L	9:14 PM	(1.74) H
9:36 AM	(1.44) H	3:16 PM	(0.61) L	9:45 PM	(1.75) H
10:14 AM	(1.38) H	3:47 PM	(0.66) L	10:19 PM	(1.73) H
10:54 AM	(1.31) H	4:20 PM	(0.71) L	10:56 PM	(1.69) H
11:39 AM	(1.26) H	4:59 PM	(0.77) L	11:40 PM	(1.64) H
12:31 PM	(1.21) H	5:47 PM	(0.82) L		
7:43 AM	(0.68) L	1:36 PM	(1.19) H	6:50 PM	(0.86) L
8:50 AM	(0.66) L	2:51 PM	(1.21) H	8:08 PM	(0.85) L
9:52 AM	(0.60) L	4:00 PM	(1.29) H	9:27 PM	(0.80) L
10:44 AM	(0.51) L	4:54 PM	(1.42) H	10:35 PM	(0.70) L
11:29 AM	(0.43) L	5:42 PM	(1.56) H	11:35 PM	(0.58) L
12:12 PM	(0.37) L	6:27 PM	(1.72) H		
6:39 AM	(1.78) H	12:54 PM	(0.34) L	7:12 PM	(1.86) H
7:31 AM	(1.75) H	1:36 PM	(0.34) L	7:58 PM	(1.98) H
8:25 AM	(1.68) H	2:19 PM	(0.39) L	8:45 PM	(2.05) H
9:20 AM	(1.59) H	3:04 PM	(0.46) L	9:32 PM	(2.07) H
10:16 AM	(1.48) H	3:52 PM	(0.55) L	10:23 PM	(2.03) H

SOLAR/LUNAR BITE TIMES

Apogee moon phase on Monday 14th

Perigee moon phase on Monday 28th

● **New moon on Monday 28th**

First quarter moon on Saturday 5th

○ **Full moon on Sunday 13th**

Last quarter moon phase on Monday 21st

Sydney, NSW: Rise: 06:17am Set: 05:32pm

Note: Daylight Savings ends (clocks turn backward 1 hour) on Sunday, 6th April at 3:00 AM.

Add 1 hour to rise/set time for days before April 7th. These sun rise/set times are averages for the month

DAY	MINOR BITE	MAJOR BITE	MINOR BITE	MAJOR BITE	SALT WATER RATING	FRESH WATER RATING
TUE 1	8:45 AM	1:48 PM	6:43 PM	1:19 AM	6	7
WED 2	10:04 AM	2:48 PM	7:27 PM	2:17 AM	5	5
THUR 3	11:18 AM	3:50 PM	8:21 PM	3:19 AM	4	6
FRI 4	12:23 PM	4:52 PM	9:23 PM	4:20 AM	3	5
SAT 5	1:16 PM	5:51 PM	10:30 PM	5:21 AM	4	6
SUN 6	1:58 PM	6:45 PM	11:38 PM	6:17 AM	5	6
MON 7	2:32 PM	7:34 PM		7:09 AM	4	5
TUE 8	3:00 PM	8:20 PM	12:44 AM	7:57 AM	3	5
WED 9	3:24 PM	9:02 PM	1:47 AM	8:41 AM	6	6
THUR 10	3:46 PM	9:42 PM	2:48 AM	9:22 AM	6	6
FRI 11	4:07 PM	10:21 PM	3:47 AM	10:01 AM	5	7

APRIL 2025
POPULAR LOCATION (See full list)
ADJUSTMENTS (on page 7)

DAY	MINOR BITE	MAJOR BITE	MINOR BITE	MAJOR BITE	SALT WATER RATING	FRESH WATER RATING
SAT 12	4:27 PM	11:00 PM	4:45 AM	10:40 AM	3	8
SUN 13	4:49 PM	11:41 PM	5:44 AM	11:20 AM	◯ 5	7
MON 14	5:14 PM		6:43 AM	12:02 PM	7	6
TUE 15	5:42 PM	12:24 AM	7:44 AM	12:46 PM	7	6
WED 16	6:16 PM	1:09 AM	8:45 AM	1:33 PM	5	5
THUR 17	6:57 PM	1:57 AM	9:46 AM	2:22 PM	4	4
FRI 18	7:45 PM	2:49 AM	10:45 AM	3:15 PM	4	4
SAT 19	8:42 PM	3:42 AM	11:38 AM	4:08 PM	3	6
SUN 20	9:46 PM	4:36 AM	12:25 PM	5:03 PM	4	4
MON 21	10:54 PM	5:30 AM	1:05 PM	5:56 PM	5	5
TUE 22		6:22 AM	1:39 PM	6:47 PM	6	6
WED 23	12:04 AM	7:12 AM	2:09 PM	7:36 PM	7	7
THUR 24	1:15 AM	8:01 AM	2:36 PM	8:25 PM	7	8
FRI 25	2:27 AM	8:50 AM	3:03 PM	9:15 PM	5	8
SAT 26	3:40 AM	9:41 AM	3:30 PM	10:07 PM	6	7
SUN 27	4:56 AM	10:33 AM	3:59 PM	11:00 PM	8	8
MON 28	6:16 AM	11:29 AM	4:34 PM	11:59 PM	● 8	8
TUE 29	7:36 AM	12:30 PM	5:16 PM		8	6
WED 30	8:55 AM	1:33 PM	6: 7 PM	1: 1 AM	7	6

TIDE TIMES

Tim Smith's

POPULAR TIDE ADJUSTMENTS

Ballina Boat Dock	+15min	Morpeth	+3hrs 10min
Batemans Bay	-1min	Moruya	+30min
Bermagui	+5min	Murwillumbah	+2hrs 30min
Blackmans Point	+1hr 15min	Narooma	+40min
Botany Bay	+3min	Nelson Bay	+30min
Broughton Island	-6min	Peats Ferry Bridge	+1hr
Byron Bay	0	Pindimar	+45min
Chinderah	+1hr 15min	Pittwater Entrance	0
Clyde River Bridge	+1hr	Port Hacking	+2min
Coffs Harbour	-2min	Port Hacking Audley	+ 30min
Como	+30min	Port Hacking Burraneer	+15min
Coraki	+4hrs	Port Hacking Lilli Pilli	+30min
Crookhaven Jetty	+15min	Port Macquarie	+21min
Crowdy Head	0	Port Stephens	0
Danger Island	+18min	Queens Lake	+2hrs
Dolls Point	+15min	Raleigh	+1hr
Ettalong	+30min	Raymond Terrace	+1hr 55min
Evans Head Bridge	0	Salamander Bay	+45min
Fig Tree Bridge	+15min	Sandon	+30min
Forster	+1min	Shoalhaven Riv' Nowra	+2hrs 10min
Gabo Island	-9min	Shoalhaven Riv'O'Keefes Pt	+2hrs
Gladesville Bridge	+15min	Silverwater Bridge	+15min
Gladstone	+2hrs 10min	Soldiers Point	+1hr
Grafton	+4hrs 1 min	South West Rocks	+1hr 2min
Greenwell Point	+45min	Swansea	-3min
Harrington	+1 min	Taree	+2hrs
Harrington Inlet	+16min	Tea Gardens	+1hr
Hexham	+1hr 10min	Terranora Inlet	+2hrs 10min
Huskisson	+3min	The Spit Bridge	0
Iluka	0	Trial Bay	0
Jervis Bay	-3min	Tweed Heads	+4min
Kempsey	+3hrs 15min	Ulladulla Harbour	0
Kendall	+3hrs 30min	Ulmarra	+4hrs 30min
Kiama	0	Wardell	+1 hr 30 min
Kurnell	0	Watson Taylors Lake	+2hrs
Lismore	+1hr 15min	Wauchope	+1hr 30min
Liverpool+	+2hrs 30min	Windsor	+5hrs 50min
Lower Portland Ferry	+3hrs 5min	Wingham	+3hrs 15min
Lugarno	+1hr	Wisemans Ferry	+1hrs 15min
Maclean	+1hr	Wollomba River mouth	+1hr 50min
Merimbula Lake Bridge	+1hr 30min	Wollongong	0
Milperra	+2hrs 10min	Wooli	+1hr 5min

Fort Denison

Day	Date	Tide 1	
THu	1	5:14 AM	(0.35) L
Fri	2	6:16 AM	(0.43) L
Sat	3	12:13 AM	(1.84) H
Sun	4	1:16 AM	(1.72) H
Mon	5	2:24 AM	(1.63) H
Tue	6	3:30 AM	(1.57) H
Wed	7	4:27 AM	(1.54) H
THu	8	5:15 AM	(1.52) H
Fri	9	12:05 AM	(0.70) L
Sat	10	12:48 AM	(0.65) L
Sun	11	1:29 AM	(0.60) L
Mon	12	2:06 AM	(0.56) L
Tue	13 ○	2:44 AM	(0.53) L
Wed	14	3:22 AM	(0.53) L
THu	15	4:01 AM	(0.54) L
Fri	16	4:44 AM	(0.56) L
Sat	17	5:30 AM	(0.59) L
Sun	18	6:21 AM	(0.61) L
Mon	19	12:10 AM	(1.70) H
Tue	20	1:07 AM	(1.67) H
Wed	21	2:11 AM	(1.65) H
THu	22	3:16 AM	(1.65) H
Fri	23	4:19 AM	(1.65) H
Sat	24	5:18 AM	(1.64) H
Sun	25	12:17 AM	(0.48) L
Mon	26	1:16 AM	(0.38) L
Tue	27 ●	2:14 AM	(0.31) L
Wed	28	3:10 AM	(0.29) L
THu	29	4:05 AM	(0.30) L
Fri	30	5:01 AM	(0.35) L
Sat	31	5:58 AM	(0.43) L

Tide 2		Tide 3		Tide 4	
11:15 AM	(1.39) H	4:43 PM	(0.65) L	11:16 PM	(1.95) H
12:17 PM	(1.31) H	5:38 PM	(0.73) L		
7:23 AM	(0.51) L	1:25 PM	(1.27) H	6:42 PM	(0.80) L
8:28 AM	(0.57) L	2:35 PM	(1.27) H	7:53 PM	(0.84) L
9:27 AM	(0.60) L	3:40 PM	(1.31) H	9:07 PM	(0.84) L
10:16 AM	(0.61) L	4:34 PM	(1.38) H	10:15 PM	(0.81) L
10:59 AM	(0.61) L	5:19 PM	(1.46) H	11:15 PM	(0.76) L
11:35 AM	(0.60) L	5:59 PM	(1.54) H		
5:59 AM	(1.50) H	12:08 PM	(0.59) L	6:34 PM	(1.62) H
6:38 AM	(1.48) H	12:38 PM	(0.59) L	7:07 PM	(1.69) H
7:17 AM	(1.46) H	1:08 PM	(0.60) L	7:39 PM	(1.75) H
7:56 AM	(1.43) H	1:38 PM	(0.61) L	8:11 PM	(1.80) H
8:35 AM	(1.41) H	2:10 PM	(0.64) L	8:44 PM	(1.82) H
9:15 AM	(1.37) H	2:44 PM	(0.67) L	9:18 PM	(1.82) H
9:56 AM	(1.34) H	3:19 PM	(0.70) L	9:56 PM	(1.81) H
10:39 AM	(1.31) H	3:59 PM	(0.74) L	10:36 PM	(1.78) H
11:25 AM	(1.28) H	4:42 PM	(0.77) L	11:20 PM	(1.74) H
12:16 PM	(1.26) H	5:33 PM	(0.80) L		
7:16 AM	(0.61) L	1:15 PM	(1.27) H	6:33 PM	(0.82) L
8:12 AM	(0.58) L	2:19 PM	(1.32) H	7:44 PM	(0.82) L
9:06 AM	(0.54) L	3:20 PM	(1.41) H	8:58 PM	(0.78) L
9:56 AM	(0.49) L	4:15 PM	(1.54) H	10:09 PM	(0.70) L
10:43 AM	(0.45) L	5:06 PM	(1.68) H	11:15 PM	(0.59) L
11:29 AM	(0.43) L	5:55 PM	(1.83) H		
6:15 AM	(1.61) H	12:15 PM	(0.43) L	6:45 PM	(1.96) H
7:14 AM	(1.57) H	1:02 PM	(0.46) L	7:34 PM	(2.05) H
8:11 AM	(1.52) H	1:50 PM	(0.50) L	8:24 PM	(2.11) H
9:09 AM	(1.47) H	2:41 PM	(0.54) L	9:15 PM	(2.11) H
10:05 AM	(1.41) H	3:32 PM	(0.60) L	10:07 PM	(2.06) H
11:02 AM	(1.37) H	4:26 PM	(0.66) L	10:59 PM	(1.97) H
11:59 AM	(1.34) H	5:21 PM	(0.72) L	11:51 PM	(1.85) H

SOLAR/LUNAR BITE TIMES

Tim Smith's

Apogee moon phase on Sunday 11th
Perigee moon phase on Monday 26th
● New moon on Tuesday 27th
First quarter moon on Sunday 4th
○ Full moon on Tuesday 13th
Last quarter moon phase on Tuesday 20th

Sydney, NSW: Rise: 06:40am Set: 05:03pm
(Note: These sun rise/set times are averages for the month)

DAY	MINOR BITE	MAJOR BITE	MINOR BITE	MAJOR BITE	SALT WATER RATING	FRESH WATER RATING
THUR 1	10:07 AM	2:38 PM	7:09 PM	2:05 AM	6	7
FRI 2	11:07 AM	3:40 PM	8:16 PM	3:08 AM	5	5
SAT 3	11:55 AM	4:38 PM	9:26 PM	4:09 AM	4	6
SUN 4	12:33 PM	5:30 PM	10:34 PM	5:03 AM	3	5
MON 5	1:04 PM	6:18 PM	11:40 PM	5:54 AM	4	6
TUE 6	1:29 PM	7:01 PM		6:39 AM	5	6
WED 7	1:51 PM	7:42 PM	12:42 AM	7:21 AM	4	5
THUR 8	2:12 PM	8:21 PM	1:41 AM	8:01 AM	3	5
FRI 9	2:33 PM	9:00 PM	2:39 AM	8:40 AM	6	6
SAT 10	2:54 PM	9:40 PM	3:37 AM	9:20 AM	5	7
SUN 11	3:18 PM	10:22 PM	4:36 AM	10:01 AM	3	8

DAY	MINOR BITE	MAJOR BITE	MINOR BITE	MAJOR BITE	SALT WATER RATING	FRESH WATER RATING
MON 12	3:45 PM	11:07 PM	5:36 AM	10:44 AM	3	8
TUE 13	4:17 PM	11:54 PM	6:38 AM	11:30 AM	○ 5	7
WED 14	4:56 PM		7:39 AM	12:19 PM	7	6
THUR 15	5:42 PM	12:45 AM	8:39 AM	1:11 PM	7	6
FRI 16	6:37 PM	1:38 AM	9:34 AM	2:05 PM	5	5
SAT 17	7:38 PM	2:32 AM	10:22 AM	2:58 PM	4	4
SUN 18	8:44 PM	3:25 AM	11:04 AM	3:50 PM	3	6
MON 19	9:51 PM	4:17 AM	11:39 AM	4:41 PM	4	4
TUE 20	11:00 PM	5:06 AM	12:10 PM	5:30 PM	5	5
WED 21		5:54 AM	12:37 PM	6:17 PM	6	6
THUR 22	12:09 AM	6:41 AM	1:03 PM	7:04 PM	7	7
FRI 23	1:19 AM	7:29 AM	1:28 PM	7:53 PM	7	8
SAT 24	2:31 AM	8:19 AM	1:56 PM	8:45 PM	5	8
SUN 25	3:47 AM	9:12 AM	2:27 PM	9:40 PM	6	7
MON 26	5:06 AM	10:09 AM	3:05 PM	10:40 PM	8	8
TUE 27	6:26 AM	11:11 AM	3:51 PM	11:44 PM	● 8	8
WED 28	7:43 AM	12:17 PM	4:49 PM		8	6
THUR 29	8:50 AM	1:22 PM	5:55 PM	12:49 AM	7	6
FRI 30	9:46 AM	2:24 PM	7:07 PM	1:53 AM	6	7
SAT 31	10:29 AM	3:20 PM	8:18 PM	2:52 AM	5	5

TIDE TIMES
Tim Smith's

POPULAR TIDE ADJUSTMENTS

Ballina Boat Dock	+15min	Morpeth	+3hrs 10min
Batemans Bay	-1min	Moruya	+30min
Bermagui	+5min	Murwillumbah	+2hrs 30min
Blackmans Point	+1hr 15min	Narooma	+40min
Botany Bay	+3min	Nelson Bay	+30min
Broughton Island	-6min	Peats Ferry Bridge	+1hr
Byron Bay	0	Pindimar	+45min
Chinderah	+1hr 15min	Pittwater Entrance	0
Clyde River Bridge	+15min	Port Hacking	+2min
Coffs Harbour	-2min	Port Hacking Audley	+ 30min
Como	+30min	Port Hacking Burraneer	+15min
Coraki	+4hrs	Port Hacking Lilli Pilli	+30min
Crookhaven Jetty	+15min	Port Macquarie	+21min
Crowdy Head	0	Port Stephens	0
Danger Island	+18min	Queens Lake	+2hrs
Dolls Point	+15min	Raleigh	+1hr
Ettalong	+30min	Raymond Terrace	+1hr 55min
Evans Head Bridge	0	Salamander Bay	+45min
Fig Tree Bridge	+15min	Sandon	+30min
Forster	+1min	Shoalhaven Riv' Nowra	+2hrs 10min
Gabo Island	-9min	Shoalhaven Riv'O'Keefes Pt	+2hrs
Gladesville Bridge	+15min	Silverwater Bridge	+15min
Gladstone	+2hrs 10min	Soldiers Point	+1hr
Grafton	+4hrs 1 min	South West Rocks	+1hr 2min
Greenwell Point	+45min	Swansea	-3min
Harrington	+1 min	Taree	+2hrs
Harrington Inlet	+16min	Tea Gardens	+1hr
Hexham	+1hr 10min	Terranora Inlet	+2hrs 10min
Huskisson	+3min	The Spit Bridge	0
Iluka	0	Trial Bay	0
Jervis Bay	-3min	Tweed Heads	+4min
Kempsey	+3hrs 15min	Ulladulla Harbour	0
Kendall	+3hrs 30min	Ulmarra	+4hrs 30min
Kiama	0	Wardell	+1 hr 30 min
Kurnell	0	Watson Taylors Lake	+2hrs
Lismore	+1hr 15min	Wauchope	+1hr 30min
Liverpool+	+2hrs 30min	Windsor	+5hrs 50min
Lower Portland Ferry	+3hrs 5min	Wingham	+3hrs 15min
Lugarno	+1hr	Wisemans Ferry	+2hrs 15min
Maclean	+2hrs 15min	Wollomba River mouth	+1hr 50min
Merimbula Lake Bridge	+1hr 30min	Wollongong	0
Milperra	+2hrs 10min	Wooli	+1hr 5min

Fort Denison

Day	Date	Tide 1	
Sun	1	6:53 AM	(0.50) L
Mon	2	12:45 AM	(1.72) H
Tue	3	1:40 AM	(1.60) H
Wed	4	2:37 AM	(1.50) H
THu	5	3:33 AM	(1.44) H
Fri	6	4:27 AM	(1.39) H
Sat	7	5:17 AM	(1.37) H
Sun	8	12:26 AM	(0.68) L
Mon	9	1:08 AM	(0.62) L
Tue	10	1:48 AM	(0.56) L
Wed	11 ◯	2:27 AM	(0.52) L
THu	12	3:06 AM	(0.50) L
Fri	13	3:45 AM	(0.49) L
Sat	14	4:28 AM	(0.50) L
Sun	15	5:11 AM	(0.50) L
Mon	16	5:57 AM	(0.50) L
Tue	17	6:44 AM	(0.50) L
Wed	18	12:41 AM	(1.70) H
THu	19	1:39 AM	(1.63) H
Fri	20	2:43 AM	(1.56) H
Sat	21	3:51 AM	(1.50) H
Sun	22	4:58 AM	(1.45) H
Mon	23	12:12 AM	(0.48) L
Tue	24	1:13 AM	(0.38) L
Wed	25 ●	2:08 AM	(0.31) L
THu	26	3:00 AM	(0.29) L
Fri	27	3:51 AM	(0.30) L
Sat	28	4:40 AM	(0.35) L
Sun	29	5:26 AM	(0.41) L
Mon	30	6:10 AM	(0.48) L

Tide 2		Tide 3		Tide 4	
12:56 PM	(1.32) **H**	6:19 PM	(0.78) L		
7:45 AM	(0.57) L	1:54 PM	(1.33) **H**	7:20 PM	(0.82) L
8:33 AM	(0.61) L	2:49 PM	(1.36) **H**	8:26 PM	(0.85) L
9:16 AM	(0.64) L	3:42 PM	(1.42) **H**	9:34 PM	(0.85) L
9:57 AM	(0.64) L	4:30 PM	(1.50) **H**	10:39 PM	(0.81) L
10:36 AM	(0.64) L	5:13 PM	(1.57) **H**	11:36 PM	(0.75) L
11:14 AM	(0.64) L	5:53 PM	(1.65) **H**		
6:05 AM	(1.35) **H**	11:50 AM	(0.65) L	6:30 PM	(1.72) **H**
6:50 AM	(1.35) **H**	12:27 PM	(0.65) L	7:07 PM	(1.77) **H**
7:33 AM	(1.35) **H**	1:03 PM	(0.66) L	7:44 PM	(1.82) **H**
8:15 AM	(1.34) **H**	1:42 PM	(0.66) L	8:20 PM	(1.85) **H**
8:57 AM	(1.34) **H**	2:20 PM	(0.67) L	8:59 PM	(1.86) **H**
9:38 AM	(1.33) **H**	3:00 PM	(0.67) L	9:39 PM	(1.86) **H**
10:22 AM	(1.32) **H**	3:44 PM	(0.68) L	10:20 PM	(1.85) **H**
11:08 AM	(1.32) **H**	4:30 PM	(0.70) L	11:03 PM	(1.81) **H**
11:57 AM	(1.34) **H**	5:21 PM	(0.72) L	11:49 PM	(1.77) **H**
12:50 PM	(1.37) **H**	6:19 PM	(0.74) L		
7:32 AM	(0.50) L	1:45 PM	(1.43) **H**	7:24 PM	(0.75) L
8:21 AM	(0.50) L	2:43 PM	(1.52) **H**	8:36 PM	(0.73) L
9:11 AM	(0.50) L	3:40 PM	(1.63) **H**	9:51 PM	(0.67) L
10:01 AM	(0.50) L	4:35 PM	(1.75) **H**	11:05 PM	(0.58) L
10:53 AM	(0.51) L	5:30 PM	(1.86) **H**		
6:02 AM	(1.43) **H**	11:46 AM	(0.52) L	6:25 PM	(1.96) **H**
7:04 AM	(1.41) **H**	12:39 PM	(0.53) L	7:18 PM	(2.04) **H**
8:02 AM	(1.41) **H**	1:32 PM	(0.53) L	8:11 PM	(2.08) **H**
8:58 AM	(1.40) **H**	2:25 PM	(0.54) L	9:01 PM	(2.07) **H**
9:49 AM	(1.39) **H**	3:17 PM	(0.57) L	9:50 PM	(2.02) **H**
10:39 AM	(1.38) **H**	4:08 PM	(0.60) L	10:37 PM	(1.92) **H**
11:28 AM	(1.37) **H**	4:58 PM	(0.65) L	11:22 PM	(1.80) **H**
12:15 PM	(1.37) **H**	5:48 PM	(0.72) L		

SOLAR/LUNAR
BITE TIMES

Tim Smith's

Apogee moon phase on Saturday 7th
Perigee moon phase on Monday 23rd
● **New moon on Wednesday 25th**
First quarter moon on Tuesday 3rd
○ **Full moon on Wednesday 11th**
Last quarter moon phase on Thursday 19th

Sydney, NSW: Rise: 05:50am Set: 04:50pm
(Note: These sun rise/set times are averages for the month)

DAY	MINOR BITE	MAJOR BITE	MINOR BITE	MAJOR BITE	SALT WATER RATING	FRESH WATER RATING
SUN 1	11:03 AM	4:11 PM	9:27 PM	3:45 AM	4	6
MON 2	11:31 AM	4:57 PM	10:32 PM	4:33 AM	3	5
TUE 3	11:55 AM	5:39 PM	11:33 PM	5:17 AM	4	6
WED 4	12:17 PM	6:19 PM		5:59 AM	5	6
THUR 5	12:37 PM	6:59 PM	12:32 AM	6:39 AM	4	5
FRI 6	12:59 PM	7:39 PM	1:30 AM	7:18 AM	3	5
SAT 7	1:22 PM	8:20 PM	2:28 AM	7:59 AM	3	5
SUN 8	1:47 PM	9:03 PM	3:28 AM	8:41 AM	6	6
MON 9	2:18 PM	9:50 PM	4:29 AM	9:26 AM	5	7
TUE 10	2:55 PM	10:40 PM	5:31 AM	10:15 AM	3	8
WED 11	3:39 PM	11:33 PM	6:32 AM	11:06 AM	○ 5	7

JUNE 2025
POPULAR LOCATION (See full list
ADJUSTMENTS (on page 7)

DAY	MINOR BITE	MAJOR BITE	MINOR BITE	MAJOR BITE	SALT WATER RATING	FRESH WATER RATING
HUR 12	4:31 PM		7:29 AM	12:00 PM	7	6
RI 13	5:31 PM	12:27 AM	8:20 AM	12:54 PM	7	6
AT 14	6:36 PM	1:21 AM	9:04 AM	1:47 PM	5	5
UN 15	7:44 PM	2:14 AM	9:41 AM	2:39 PM	4	4
1ON 16	8:52 PM	3:04 AM	10:12 AM	3:28 PM	4	4
UE 17	9:59 PM	3:52 AM	10:40 AM	4:15 PM	3	6
/ED 18	11:07 PM	4:38 AM	11:05 AM	5:00 PM	4	4
HUR 19		5:24 AM	11:30 AM	5:47 PM	5	5
RI 20	12:17 AM	6:11 AM	11:56 AM	6:36 PM	6	6
AT 21	1:28 AM	7:01 AM	12:25 PM	7:27 PM	7	7
UN 22	2:43 AM	7:55 AM	12:58 PM	8:23 PM	7	8
1ON 23	4:01 AM	8:53 AM	1:40 PM	9:24 PM	6	7
UE 24	5:18 AM	9:56 AM	2:31 PM	10:28 PM	0	8
/ED 25	6:30 AM	11:01 AM	3:33 PM	11:33 PM	● 8	8
HUR 26	7:31 AM	12:05 PM	4:43 PM		8	6
RI 27	8:20 AM	1:05 PM	5:57 PM	12:35 AM	7	6
AT 28	8:59 AM	2:00 PM	7:08 PM	1:32 AM	6	7
UN 29	9:30 AM	2:49 PM	8:16 PM	2:24 AM	6	7
1ON 30	9:56 AM	3:34 PM	9:2 PM	3:11 AM	5	5

TIDE TIMES

Tim Smith's

POPULAR TIDE ADJUSTMENTS

Ballina Boat Dock	+15min	Morpeth	+3hrs 10min
Batemans Bay	-1min	Moruya	+30min
Bermagui	+5min	Murwillumbah	+2hrs 30min
Blackmans Point	+1hr 15min	Narooma	+40min
Botany Bay	+3min	Nelson Bay	+30min
Broughton Island	-6min	Peats Ferry Bridge	+1hr
Byron Bay	0	Pindimar	+45min
Chinderah	+1hr 15min	Pittwater Entrance	0
Clyde River Bridge	+15min	Port Hacking	+2min
Coffs Harbour	-2min	Port Hacking Audley	+ 30min
Como	+30min	Port Hacking Burraneer	+15min
Coraki	+4hrs	Port Hacking Lilli Pilli	+30min
Crookhaven Jetty	+15min	Port Macquarie	+21min
Crowdy Head	0	Port Stephens	0
Danger Island	+18min	Queens Lake	+2hrs
Dolls Point	+15min	Raleigh	+1hr
Ettalong	+30min	Raymond Terrace	+1hr 55min
Evans Head Bridge	0	Salamander Bay	+45min
Fig Tree Bridge	+15min	Sandon	+30min
Forster	+1min	Shoalhaven Riv' Nowra	+2hrs 10min
Gabo Island	-9min	Shoalhaven Riv'O'Keefes Pt	+2hrs
Gladesville Bridge	+15min	Silverwater Bridge	+15min
Gladstone	+2hrs 10min	Soldiers Point	+1hr
Grafton	+4hrs 1 min	South West Rocks	+1hr 2min
Greenwell Point	+45min	Swansea	-3min
Harrington	+1 min	Taree	+2hrs
Harrington Inlet	+16min	Tea Gardens	+1hr
Hexham	+1hr 10min	Terranora Inlet	+2hrs 10min
Huskisson	+3min	The Spit Bridge	0
Iluka	0	Trial Bay	0
Jervis Bay	-3min	Tweed Heads	+4min
Kempsey	+3hrs 15min	Ulladulla Harbour	0
Kendall	+3hrs 30min	Ulmarra	+4hrs 30min
Kiama	0	Wardell	+1 hr 30 min
Kurnell	0	Watson Taylors Lake	+2hrs
Lismore	+1hr 15min	Wauchope	+1hr 30min
Liverpool+	+2hrs 30min	Windsor	+5hrs 50min
Lower Portland Ferry	+3hrs 5min	Wingham	+3hrs 15min
Lugarno	+1hr	Wisemans Ferry	+2hrs 15min
Maclean	+2hrs 15min	Wollomba River mouth	+1hr 50min
Merimbula Lake Bridge	+1hr 30min	Wollongong	0
Milperra	+2hrs 10min	Wooli	+1hr 5min

Fort Denison

Day	Date	Tide 1		
Tue	1	12:05 AM	(1.67)	**H**
Wed	2	12:49 AM	(1.53)	**H**
THu	3	1:38 AM	(1.41)	**H**
Fri	4	2:34 AM	(1.32)	**H**
Sat	5	3:37 AM	(1.26)	**H**
Sun	6	4:40 AM	(1.23)	**H**
Mon	7	12:02 AM	(0.68)	L
Tue	8	12:49 AM	(0.60)	L
Wed	9	1:30 AM	(0.53)	L
THu	10	2:09 AM	(0.48)	L
Fri	11 ○	2:47 AM	(0.43)	L
Sat	12	3:26 AM	(0.40)	L
Sun	13	4:04 AM	(0.38)	L
Mon	14	4:45 AM	(0.37)	L
Tue	15	5:26 AM	(0.38)	L
Wed	16	6:09 AM	(0.40)	L
THu	17	12:18 AM	(1.65)	**H**
Fri	18	1:14 AM	(1.51)	**H**
Sat	19	2:20 AM	(1.39)	**H**
Sun	20	3:36 AM	(1.31)	**H**
Mon	21	4:53 AM	(1.28)	**H**
Tue	22	12:13 AM	(0.45)	L
Wed	23	1:10 AM	(0.36)	L
THu	24	2:00 AM	(0.30)	L
Fri	25 ●	2:46 AM	(0.28)	L
Sat	26	3:29 AM	(0.29)	L
Sun	27	4:08 AM	(0.33)	L
Mon	28	4:45 AM	(0.38)	L
Tue	29	5:19 AM	(0.45)	L
Wed	30	5:51 AM	(0.51)	L
THu	31	12:02 AM	(1.44)	**H**

Tide 2		Tide 3		Tide 4	
6:51 AM	(0.55) L	1:03 PM	(1.38) H	6:42 PM	(0.78) L
7:30 AM	(0.60) L	1:53 PM	(1.40) H	7:41 PM	(0.82) L
8:10 AM	(0.63) L	2:43 PM	(1.44) H	8:48 PM	(0.84) L
8:51 AM	(0.66) L	3:34 PM	(1.49) H	10:00 PM	(0.81) L
9:37 AM	(0.68) L	4:25 PM	(1.55) H	11:07 PM	(0.76) L
10:24 AM	(0.69) L	5:13 PM	(1.61) H		
5:38 AM	(1.24) H	11:11 AM	(0.68) L	5:58 PM	(1.68) H
6:30 AM	(1.25) H	11:57 AM	(0.67) L	6:40 PM	(1.74) H
7:15 AM	(1.28) H	12:40 PM	(0.65) L	7:21 PM	(1.80) H
7:57 AM	(1.30) H	1:22 PM	(0.62) L	8:01 PM	(1.85) H
8:37 AM	(1.33) H	2:03 PM	(0.59) L	8:41 PM	(1.89) H
9:18 AM	(1.35) H	2:46 PM	(0.57) L	9:21 PM	(1.91) H
10:00 AM	(1.38) H	3:31 PM	(0.56) L	10:02 PM	(1.89) H
10:45 AM	(1.41) H	4:18 PM	(0.57) L	10:45 PM	(1.84) H
11:32 AM	(1.44) H	5:10 PM	(0.59) L	11:30 PM	(1.76) H
12:21 PM	(1.49) H	6:07 PM	(0.63) L		
6:52 AM	(0.44) L	1:14 PM	(1.54) H	7:11 PM	(0.65) L
7:40 AM	(0.49) L	2:10 PM	(1.59) H	8:24 PM	(0.66) L
8:31 AM	(0.53) L	3:11 PM	(1.66) H	9:45 PM	(0.63) L
9:30 AM	(0.57) L	4:14 PM	(1.73) H	11:05 PM	(0.55) L
10:31 AM	(0.58) L	5:15 PM	(1.82) H		
6:02 AM	(1.29) H	11:32 AM	(0.57) L	6:15 PM	(1.90) H
7:02 AM	(1.32) H	12:30 PM	(0.53) L	7:09 PM	(1.96) H
7:54 AM	(1.36) H	1:24 PM	(0.50) L	8:00 PM	(1.99) H
8:42 AM	(1.39) H	2:14 PM	(0.48) L	8:46 PM	(1.98) H
9:26 AM	(1.41) H	3:00 PM	(0.49) L	9:30 PM	(1.92) H
10:09 AM	(1.42) H	3:46 PM	(0.52) L	10:10 PM	(1.82) H
10:50 AM	(1.42) H	4:30 PM	(0.57) L	10:47 PM	(1.70) H
11:30 AM	(1.42) H	5:15 PM	(0.63) L	11:24 PM	(1.57) H
12:11 PM	(1.43) H	6:03 PM	(0.70) L		
6:24 AM	(0.57) L	12:54 PM	(1.44) H	6:58 PM	(0.75) L

SOLAR/LUNAR BITE TIMES

Tim Smith's

Apogee moon phase on Saturday 5th
Perigee moon phase on Sunday 20th
● New moon on Friday 25th
First quarter moon on Thursday 3rd
○ Full moon on Friday 11th
Last quarter moon phase on Friday 18th

Sydney, NSW: Rise: 06:50am Set: 05:00pm
(Note: These sun rise/set times are averages for the month)

DAY	MINOR BITE	MAJOR BITE	MINOR BITE	MAJOR BITE	SALT WATER RATING	FRESH WATER RATING
TUE 1	10:19 AM	4:15 PM	10:21 PM	3:54 AM	4	6
WED 2	10:40 AM	4:56 PM	11:20 PM	4:35 AM	3	5
THUR 3	11:02 AM	5:35 PM		5:15 AM	4	6
FRI 4	11:24 AM	6:16 PM	12:19 AM	5:55 AM	5	6
SAT 5	11:49 AM	6:59 PM	1:18 AM	6:37 AM	4	5
SUN 6	12:18 PM	7:45 PM	2:19 AM	7:21 AM	3	5
MON 7	12:52 PM	8:33 PM	3:21 AM	8:09 AM	6	6
TUE 8	1:33 PM	9:25 PM	4:22 AM	8:58 AM	5	7
WED 9	2:23 PM	10:20 PM	5:21 AM	9:52 AM	5	7
THUR 10	3:22 PM	11:14 PM	6:14 AM	10:46 AM	3	8
FRI 11	4:26 PM		7:01 AM	11:41 AM	○ 5	7

DAY	MINOR BITE	MAJOR BITE	MINOR BITE	MAJOR BITE	SALT WATER RATING	FRESH WATER RATING
AT 12	5:34 PM	12:08 AM	7:41 AM	12:33 PM	7	6
UN 13	6:43 PM	1:00 AM	8:15 AM	1:24 PM	7	6
ON 14	7:52 PM	1:49 AM	8:44 AM	2:13 PM	5	5
UE 15	9:00 PM	2:37 AM	9:10 AM	3:00 PM	4	4
VED 16	10:08 PM	3:23 AM	9:34 AM	3:46 PM	3	6
HUR 17	11:18 PM	4:09 AM	9:59 AM	4:33 PM	4	4
RI 18		4:57 AM	10:26 AM	5:22 PM	5	5
AT 19	12:31 AM	5:48 AM	10:57 AM	6:15 PM	6	6
UN 20	1:46 AM	6:44 AM	11:35 AM	7:13 PM	7	7
ON 21	3:01 AM	7:43 AM	12:21 PM	8:14 PM	7	8
UE 22	4:13 AM	8:46 AM	1:17 PM	9:17 PM	5	8
VED 23	5:18 AM	9:49 AM	2:23 PM	10:19 PM	6	7
HUR 24	6:11 AM	10:50 AM	3:35 PM	11:18 PM	8	8
RI 25	6:54 AM	11:47 AM	4:47 PM		● 8	8
AT 26	7:28 AM	12:39 PM	5:57 PM	12:13 AM	8	6
UN 27	7:56 AM	1:26 PM	7:04 PM	1:02 AM	7	6
ON 28	8:20 AM	2:09 PM	8:07 PM	1:47 AM	6	7
UE 29	8:43 AM	2:50 PM	9:08 PM	2:29 AM	5	5
VED 30	9:04 AM	3:31 PM	10:07 PM	3:10 AM	4	6
HUR 31	9:26 AM	4:11 PM	11:07 PM	3:51 AM	3	5

TIDE TIMES

Tim Smith's TIMES

POPULAR TIDE ADJUSTMENTS

Ballina Boat Dock	+15min	Morpeth	+3hrs 10min
Batemans Bay	-1min	Moruya	+30min
Bermagui	+5min	Murwillumbah	+2hrs 30min
Blackmans Point	+1hr 15min	Narooma	+40min
Botany Bay	+3min	Nelson Bay	+30min
Broughton Island	-6min	Peats Ferry Bridge	+1hr
Byron Bay	0	Pindimar	+45min
Chinderah	+1hr 15min	Pittwater Entrance	0
Clyde River Bridge	+15min	Port Hacking	+2min
Coffs Harbour	-2min	Port Hacking Audley	+30min
Como	+30min	Port Hacking Burraneer	+15min
Coraki	+4hrs	Port Hacking Lilli Pilli	+30min
Crookhaven Jetty	+15min	Port Macquarie	+21min
Crowdy Head	0	Port Stephens	0
Danger Island	+18min	Queens Lake	+2hrs
Dolls Point	+15min	Raleigh	+1hr
Ettalong	+30min	Raymond Terrace	+1hr 55min
Evans Head Bridge	0	Salamander Bay	+45min
Fig Tree Bridge	+15min	Sandon	+30min
Forster	+1min	Shoalhaven Riv' Nowra	+2hrs 10min
Gabo Island	-9min	Shoalhaven Riv'O'Keefes Pt	+2hrs
Gladesville Bridge	+15min	Silverwater Bridge	+15min
Gladstone	+2hrs 10min	Soldiers Point	+1hr
Grafton	+4hrs 1 min	South West Rocks	+1hr 2min
Greenwell Point	+45min	Swansea	-3min
Harrington	+1 min	Taree	+2hrs
Harrington Inlet	+16min	Tea Gardens	+1hr
Hexham	+1hr 10min	Terranora Inlet	+2hrs 10min
Huskisson	+3min	The Spit Bridge	0
Iluka	0	Trial Bay	0
Jervis Bay	-3min	Tweed Heads	+4min
Kempsey	+3hrs 15min	Ulladulla Harbour	0
Kendall	+3hrs 30min	Ulmarra	+4hrs 30min
Kiama	0	Wardell	+1 hr 30 min
Kurnell	0	Watson Taylors Lake	+2hrs
Lismore	+1hr 15min	Wauchope	+1hr 30min
Liverpool+	+2hrs 30min	Windsor	+5hrs 50min
Lower Portland Ferry	+3hrs 5min	Wingham	+3hrs 15min
Lugarno	+1hr	Wisemans Ferry	+2hrs 15min
Maclean	+2hrs 15min	Wollomba River mouth	+1hr 50min
Merimbula Lake Bridge	+1hr 30min	Wollongong	0
Milperra	+2hrs 10min	Wooli	+1hr 5min

Fort Denison

Day	Date	Tide 1	
Fri	1	12:45 AM	(1.32) **H**
Sat	2	1:41 AM	(1.22) **H**
Sun	3	2:51 AM	(1.15) **H**
Mon	4	4:09 AM	(1.13) **H**
Tue	5	5:17 AM	(1.15) **H**
Wed	6	12:27 AM	(0.56) **L**
THu	7	1:08 AM	(0.48) **L**
Fri	8	1:45 AM	(0.40) **L**
Sat	9 ◯	2:21 AM	(0.33) **L**
Sun	10	2:58 AM	(0.28) **L**
Mon	11	3:34 AM	(0.25) **L**
Tue	12	4:13 AM	(0.26) **L**
Wed	13	4:51 AM	(0.29) **L**
THu	14	5:31 AM	(0.35) **L**
Fri	15	12:01 AM	(1.51) **H**
Sat	16	1:00 AM	(1.35) **H**
Sun	17	2:13 AM	(1.23) **H**
Mon	18	3:40 AM	(1.17) **H**
Tue	19	5:01 AM	(1.18) **H**
Wed	20	12:10 AM	(0.41) **L**
THu	21	1:00 AM	(0.34) **L**
Fri	22	1:44 AM	(0.30) **L**
Sat	23 ●	2:22 AM	(0.28) **L**
Sun	24	2:57 AM	(0.29) **L**
Mon	25	3:29 AM	(0.33) **L**
Tue	26	3:59 AM	(0.38) **L**
Wed	27	4:27 AM	(0.43) **L**
THu	28	4:54 AM	(0.50) **L**
Fri	29	5:24 AM	(0.56) **L**
Sat	30	12:07 AM	(1.24) **H**
Sun	31	1:01 AM	(1.14) **H**

Tide 2		Tide 3		Tide 4	
7:00 AM	(0.62) L	1:42 PM	(1.45) **H**	8:02 PM	(0.78) L
7:45 AM	(0.67) L	2:36 PM	(1.46) **H**	9:19 PM	(0.78) L
8:40 AM	(0.71) L	3:36 PM	(1.49) **H**	10:35 PM	(0.73) L
9:42 AM	(0.72) L	4:35 PM	(1.54) **H**	11:38 PM	(0.65) L
10:41 AM	(0.70) L	5:29 PM	(1.61) **H**		
6:11 AM	(1.20) **H**	11:34 AM	(0.66) L	6:16 PM	(1.69) **H**
6:55 AM	(1.25) **H**	12:21 PM	(0.60) L	6:59 PM	(1.77) **H**
7:34 AM	(1.31) **H**	1:04 PM	(0.53) L	7:39 PM	(1.85) **H**
8:14 AM	(1.37) **H**	1:47 PM	(0.47) L	8:19 PM	(1.90) **H**
8:54 AM	(1.43) **H**	2:31 PM	(0.43) L	9:00 PM	(1.91) **H**
9:35 AM	(1.49) **H**	3:18 PM	(0.41) L	9:42 PM	(1.88) **H**
10:18 AM	(1.54) **H**	4:07 PM	(0.42) L	10:25 PM	(1.80) **H**
11:03 AM	(1.59) **H**	5:00 PM	(0.45) L	11:11 PM	(1.67) **H**
11:52 AM	(1.62) **H**	5:58 PM	(0.50) L		
6:15 AM	(0.44) L	12:44 PM	(1.63) **H**	7:04 PM	(0.56) L
7:04 AM	(0.53) L	1:43 PM	(1.63) **H**	8:22 PM	(0.58) L
8:03 AM	(0.60) L	2:50 PM	(1.65) **H**	9:49 PM	(0.56) L
9:14 AM	(0.64) L	4:02 PM	(1.68) **H**	11:08 PM	(0.50) L
10:26 AM	(0.62) L	5:10 PM	(1.74) **H**		
6:05 AM	(1.24) **H**	11:30 AM	(0.57) L	6:09 PM	(1.81) **H**
6:56 AM	(1.31) **H**	12:27 PM	(0.50) L	7:00 PM	(1.86) **H**
7:40 AM	(1.38) **H**	1:16 PM	(0.45) L	7:45 PM	(1.87) **H**
8:20 AM	(1.43) **H**	2:01 PM	(0.42) L	8:25 PM	(1.84) **H**
8:58 AM	(1.46) **H**	2:44 PM	(0.43) L	9:03 PM	(1.77) **H**
9:34 AM	(1.49) **H**	3:24 PM	(0.46) L	9:39 PM	(1.68) **H**
10:10 AM	(1.50) **H**	4:04 PM	(0.50) L	10:13 PM	(1.57) **H**
10:45 AM	(1.51) **H**	4:46 PM	(0.55) L	10:47 PM	(1.46) **H**
11:20 AM	(1.50) **H**	5:30 PM	(0.61) L	11:25 PM	(1.34) **H**
12:00 PM	(1.49) **H**	6:21 PM	(0.66) L		
6:00 AM	(0.63) L	12:45 PM	(1.47) **H**	7:21 PM	(0.71) L
6:45 AM	(0.70) L	1:39 PM	(1.44) **H**	8:37 PM	(0.72) L

SOLAR/LUNAR BITE TIMES

Apogee moon phase on Saturday 2nd and Saturday 30th
Perigee moon phase on Friday 15th
● **New moon on Saturday 23rd**
First quarter moon on Friday 1st and Sunday 31st
○ **Full moon on Saturday 9th**
Last quarter moon phase on Saturday 16th

Sydney, NSW: Rise: 06:30am Set: 05:20pm
(Note: These sun rise/set times are averages for the month)

DAY	MINOR BITE	MAJOR BITE	MINOR BITE	MAJOR BITE	SALT WATER RATING	FRESH WATER RATING
FRI 1	9:50 AM	4:53 PM		4:31 AM	4	6
SAT 2	10:17 AM	5:38 PM	12:07 AM	5:15 AM	4	6
SUN 3	10:49 AM	6:25 PM	1:09 AM	6:01 AM	5	6
MON 4	11:27 AM	7:16 PM	2:10 AM	6:50 AM	4	5
TUE 5	12:13 PM	8:09 PM	3:10 AM	7:42 AM	3	5
WED 6	1:08 PM	9:04 PM	4:06 AM	8:36 AM	6	6
THUR 7	2:11 PM	9:59 PM	4:55 AM	9:31 AM	5	7
FRI 8	3:19 PM	10:52 PM	5:38 AM	10:25 AM	3	8
SAT 9	4:29 PM	11:43 PM	6:14 AM	11:17 AM	○ 5	7
SUN 10	5:39 PM		6:45 AM	12:07 PM	7	6
MON 11	6:49 PM	12:32 AM	7:13 AM	12:55 PM	7	6

AUGUST 2025

POPULAR LOCATION ADJUSTMENTS (See full list on page 7)

DAY	MINOR BITE	MAJOR BITE	MINOR BITE	MAJOR BITE	SALT WATER RATING	FRESH WATER RATING
TUE 12	7:59 PM	1:19 AM	7:38 AM	1:43 PM	5	5
WED 13	9:09 PM	2:07 AM	8:03 AM	2:31 PM	4	4
THUR 14	10:22 PM	2:55 AM	8:30 AM	3:20 PM	3	6
FRI 15	11:36 PM	3:45 AM	8:59 AM	4:11 PM	4	4
SAT 16		4:39 AM	9:34 AM	5:07 PM	5	5
SUN 17	12:51 AM	5:36 AM	10:17 AM	6:06 PM	6	6
MON 18	2:03 AM	6:37 AM	11:09 AM	7:07 PM	7	7
TUE 19	3:09 AM	7:39 AM	12:10 PM	8:09 PM	7	8
WED 20	4:05 AM	8:40 AM	1:19 PM	9:08 PM	5	8
THUR 21	4:50 AM	9:37 AM	2:30 PM	10:03 PM	6	7
FRI 22	5:27 AM	10:30 AM	3:41 PM	10:53 PM	8	8
SAT 23	5:57 AM	11:18 AM	4:48 PM	11:40 PM	● 8	8
SUN 24	6:22 AM	12:03 PM	5:52 PM		8	6
MON 25	6:45 AM	12:45 PM	6:54 PM	12:24 AM	7	6
TUE 26	7:07 AM	1:26 PM	7:55 PM	1:05 AM	7	6
WED 27	7:28 AM	2:06 PM	8:55 PM	1:46 AM	6	7
THUR 28	7:51 AM	2:48 PM	9:55 PM	2:27 AM	5	5
FRI 29	8:17 AM	3:32 PM	10:56 PM	3:09 AM	4	6
SAT 30	8:47 AM	4:18 PM	11:57 PM	3:54 AM	3	5
SUN 31	9:22 AM	5:07 PM		4:42 AM	4	6

TIDE
Tim Smith's TIMES

POPULAR TIDE ADJUSTMENTS

Ballina Boat Dock	+15min	Morpeth	+3hrs 10min
Batemans Bay	-1min	Moruya	+30min
Bermagui	+5min	Murwillumbah	+2hrs 30min
Blackmans Point	+1hr 15min	Narooma	+40min
Botany Bay	+3min	Nelson Bay	+30min
Broughton Island	-6min	Peats Ferry Bridge	+1hr
Byron Bay	0	Pindimar	+45min
Chinderah	+1hr 15min	Pittwater Entrance	0
Clyde River Bridge	+15min	Port Hacking	+2min
Coffs Harbour	-2min	Port Hacking Audley	+ 30min
Como	+30min	Port Hacking Burraneer	+15min
Coraki	+4hrs	Port Hacking Lilli Pilli	+30min
Crookhaven Jetty	+15min	Port Macquarie	+21min
Crowdy Head	0	Port Stephens	0
Danger Island	+18min	Queens Lake	+2hrs
Dolls Point	+15min	Raleigh	+1hr
Ettalong	+30min	Raymond Terrace	+1hr 55min
Evans Head Bridge	0	Salamander Bay	+45min
Fig Tree Bridge	+15min	Sandon	+30min
Forster	+1min	Shoalhaven Riv' Nowra	+2hrs 10min
Gabo Island	-9min	Shoalhaven Riv'O'Keefes Pt	+2hrs
Gladesville Bridge	+15min	Silverwater Bridge	+15min
Gladstone	+2hrs 10min	Soldiers Point	+1hr
Grafton	+4hrs 1 min	South West Rocks	+1hr 2min
Greenwell Point	+45min	Swansea	-3min
Harrington	+1 min	Taree	+2hrs
Harrington Inlet	+16min	Tea Gardens	+1hr
Hexham	+1hr 10min	Terranora Inlet	+2hrs 10min
Huskisson	+3min	The Spit Bridge	0
Iluka	0	Trial Bay	0
Jervis Bay	-3min	Tweed Heads	+4min
Kempsey	+3hrs 15min	Ulladulla Harbour	0
Kendall	+3hrs 30min	Ulmarra	+4hrs 30min
Kiama	0	Wardell	+1 hr 30 min
Kurnell	0	Watson Taylors Lake	+3hrs
Lismore	+1hr 15min	Wauchope	+1hr 30min
Liverpool+	+2hrs 30min	Windsor	+5hrs 50min
Lower Portland Ferry	+3hrs 5min	Wingham	+3hrs 15min
Lugarno	+1hr	Wisemans Ferry	+2hrs 15min
Maclean	+2hrs 15min	Wollomba River mouth	+1hr 50min
Merimbula Lake Bridge	+1hr 30min	Wollongong	0
Milperra	+2hrs 10min	Wooli	+1hr 5min

Day	Date		Tide 1	
Mon	1		2:14 AM	(1.08) H
Tue	2		3:40 AM	(1.07) H
Wed	3		4:53 AM	(1.12) H
THu	4		5:45 AM	(1.19) H
Fri	5		12:35 AM	(0.43) L
Sat	6		1:12 AM	(0.33) L
Sun	7		1:46 AM	(0.26) L
Mon	8	○	2:22 AM	(0.21) L
Tue	9		2:59 AM	(0.19) L
Wed	10		3:37 AM	(0.22) L
THu	11		4:16 AM	(0.29) L
Fri	12		4:59 AM	(0.38) L
Sat	13		5:45 AM	(0.49) L
Sun	14		12:59 AM	(1.23) H
Mon	15		2:20 AM	(1.14) H
Tue	16		3:50 AM	(1.14) H
Wed	17		5:01 AM	(1.20) H
THu	18		5:54 AM	(1.28) H
Fri	19		12:37 AM	(0.36) L
Sat	20		1:15 AM	(0.33) L
Sun	21		1:47 AM	(0.33) L
Mon	22	●	2:17 AM	(0.34) L
Tue	23		2:45 AM	(0.37) L
Wed	24		3:11 AM	(0.42) L
THu	25		3:37 AM	(0.47) L
Fri	26		4:05 AM	(0.53) L
Sat	27		4:37 AM	(0.59) L
Sun	28		5:15 AM	(0.66) L
Mon	29		12:35 AM	(1.12) H
Tue	30		1:44 AM	(1.08) H

SEPTEMBER 2025

Tide 2		Tide 3		Tide 4	
7:47 AM	(0.74) L	2:45 PM	(1.44) H	9:58 PM	(0.69) L
9:02 AM	(0.75) L	3:56 PM	(1.47) H	11:04 PM	(0.62) L
10:13 AM	(0.72) L	4:57 PM	(1.55) H	11:54 PM	(0.53) L
11:11 AM	(0.64) L	5:47 PM	(1.65) H		
6:28 AM	(1.28) H	12:00 PM	(0.55) L	6:30 PM	(1.74) H
7:07 AM	(1.37) H	12:45 PM	(0.45) L	7:12 PM	(1.82) H
7:45 AM	(1.47) H	1:30 PM	(0.37) L	7:53 PM	(1.87) H
8:25 AM	(1.57) H	2:17 PM	(0.31) L	8:36 PM	(1.86) H
9:07 AM	(1.66) H	3:06 PM	(0.29) L	9:20 PM	(1.79) H
9:50 AM	(1.72) H	3:58 PM	(0.29) L	10:07 PM	(1.68) H
10:36 AM	(1.75) H	4:53 PM	(0.33) L	10:58 PM	(1.53) H
11:25 AM	(1.75) H	5:54 PM	(0.40) L	11:53 PM	(1.37) H
12:19 PM	(1.71) H	7:03 PM	(0.47) L		
6:40 AM	(0.60) L	1:22 PM	(1.66) H	8:25 PM	(0.51) L
7:49 AM	(0.67) L	2:36 PM	(1.63) H	9:48 PM	(0.50) L
9:10 AM	(0.68) L	3:54 PM	(1.63) H	10:59 PM	(0.46) L
10:26 AM	(0.64) L	5:01 PM	(1.67) H	11:54 PM	(0.40) L
11:28 AM	(0.56) L	5:56 PM	(1.71) H		
6:38 AM	(1.37) H	12:20 PM	(0.49) L	6:42 PM	(1.72) H
7:16 AM	(1.44) H	1:05 PM	(0.44) L	7:22 PM	(1.71) H
7:53 AM	(1.51) H	1:47 PM	(0.42) L	8:00 PM	(1.67) H
8:27 AM	(1.55) H	2:26 PM	(0.41) L	8:34 PM	(1.61) H
8:59 AM	(1.58) H	3:04 PM	(0.42) L	9:08 PM	(1.53) H
9:30 AM	(1.61) H	3:43 PM	(0.45) L	9:43 PM	(1.45) H
10:02 AM	(1.61) H	4:22 PM	(0.49) L	10:19 PM	(1.36) H
10:36 AM	(1.59) H	5:04 PM	(0.53) L	10:58 PM	(1.28) H
11:14 AM	(1.56) H	5:51 PM	(0.59) L	11:42 PM	(1.19) H
11:57 AM	(1.51) H	6:47 PM	(0.64) L		
6:01 AM	(0.73) L	12:49 PM	(1.46) H	7:57 PM	(0.67) L
7:05 AM	(0.77) L	1:56 PM	(1.44) H	9:14 PM	(0.65) L

SOLAR/LUNAR BITE TIMES

Tim Smith's

Apogee moon phase on Friday 26th
Perigee moon phase on Wednesday 10th
● New moon on Monday 22nd
First quarter moon on Monday 29th
○ Full moon on Monday 8th
Last quarter moon phase on Sunday 14th

Sydney, NSW: Rise: 05:50am Set: 05:40pm
(Note: These sun rise/set times are averages for the month)

DAY	MINOR BITE	MAJOR BITE	MINOR BITE	MAJOR BITE	SALT WATER RATING	FRESH WATER RATING
MON 1	10:05 AM	5:58 PM	12:57 PM	5:32 AM	5	6
TUE 2	10:55 AM	6:52 PM	1:55 AM	6:25 AM	4	5
WED 3	11:54 AM	7:46 PM	2:47 AM	7:18 AM	3	5
THUR 4	12:59 PM	8:40 PM	3:32 AM	8:13 AM	6	6
FRI 5	2:08 PM	9:32 PM	4:10 AM	9:05 AM	5	7
SAT 6	3:19 PM	10:22 PM	4:44 AM	9:56 AM	5	7
SUN 7	4:30 PM	11:11 PM	5:13 AM	10:46 AM	3	8
MON 8	5:42 PM	11:59 PM	5:39 AM	11:35 AM	○ 5	7
TUE 9	6:54 PM		6:05 AM	12:23 PM	7	6
WED 10	8:08 PM	12:48 AM	6:32 AM	1:13 PM	7	6
THUR 11	9:24 PM	1:39 AM	7:01 AM	2:05 PM	5	5

SEPTEMBER 2025

POPULAR LOCATION ADJUSTMENTS (See full list on page 7)

DAY	MINOR BITE	MAJOR BITE	MINOR BITE	MAJOR BITE	SALT WATER RATING	FRESH WATER RATING
FRI 12	10:40 PM	2:33 AM	7:34 AM	3:01 PM	3	6
SAT 13	11:55 PM	3:31 AM	8:15 AM	4:00 PM	4	4
SUN 14		4:31 AM	9:05 AM	5:02 PM	5	5
MON 15	1:03 AM	5:33 AM	10:03 AM	6:03 PM	6	6
TUE 16	2:02 AM	6:34 AM	11:10 AM	7:03 PM	7	7
WED 17	2:50 AM	7:32 AM	12:20 PM	7:58 PM	7	8
THUR 18	3:28 AM	8:25 AM	1:29 PM	8:49 PM	7	8
FRI 19	3:59 AM	9:14 AM	2:37 PM	9:36 PM	5	8
SAT 20	4:26 AM	9:59 AM	3:41 PM	10:19 PM	6	7
SUN 21	4:49 AM	10:41 AM	4:43 PM	11:01 PM	8	8
MON 22	5:11 AM	11:22 AM	5:44 PM	11:42 PM	● 8	8
TUE 23	5:32 AM	12:03 PM	6:44 PM		8	6
WED 24	5:55 AM	12:44 PM	7:44 PM	12:23 AM	7	6
THUR 25	6:19 AM	1:27 PM	8:45 PM	1:05 AM	6	7
FRI 26	6:47 AM	2:12 PM	9:46 PM	1:49 AM	5	5
SAT 27	7:20 AM	2:59 PM	10:46 PM	2:35 AM	4	6
SUN 28	7:59 AM	3:50 PM	11:44 PM	3:24 AM	4	6
MON 29	8:46 AM	4:42 PM		4:15 AM	3	5
TUE 30	9:40 AM	5:35 PM	12:38 AM	5:08 AM	4	6

TIDE
Tim Smith's TIMES

Fort Denison

POPULAR TIDE ADJUSTMENTS

Ballina Boat Dock	+15min	Morpeth	+3hrs 10min
Batemans Bay	-1min	Moruya	+30min
Bermagui	+5min	Murwillumbah	+2hrs 30min
Blackmans Point	+1hr 15min	Narooma	+40min
Botany Bay	+3min	Nelson Bay	+30min
Broughton Island	-6min	Peats Ferry Bridge	+1hr
Byron Bay	0	Pindimar	+45min
Chinderah	+1hr 15min	Pittwater Entrance	0
Clyde River Bridge	+15min	Port Hacking	+2min
Coffs Harbour	-2min	Port Hacking Audley	+ 30min
Como	+30min	Port Hacking Burraneer	+15min
Coraki	+4hrs	Port Hacking Lilli Pilli	+30min
Crookhaven Jetty	+15min	Port Macquarie	+21min
Crowdy Head	0	Port Stephens	0
Danger Island	+18min	Queens Lake	+2hrs
Dolls Point	+15min	Raleigh	+1hr
Ettalong	+30min	Raymond Terrace	+1hr 55min
Evans Head Bridge	0	Salamander Bay	+45min
Fig Tree Bridge	+15min	Sandon	+30min
Forster	+1min	Shoalhaven Riv' Nowra	+2hrs 10min
Gabo Island	-9min	Shoalhaven Riv'O'Keefes Pt	+2hrs
Gladesville Bridge	+15min	Silverwater Bridge	+15min
Gladstone	+2hrs 10min	Soldiers Point	+1hr
Grafton	+4hrs 1 min	South West Rocks	+1hr 2min
Greenwell Point	+45min	Swansea	-3min
Harrington	+1 min	Taree	+2hrs
Harrington Inlet	+16min	Tea Gardens	+1hr
Hexham	+1hr 10min	Terranora Inlet	+2hrs 10min
Huskisson	+3min	The Spit Bridge	0
Iluka	0	Trial Bay	0
Jervis Bay	-3min	Tweed Heads	+4min
Kempsey	+3hrs 15min	Ulladulla Harbour	0
Kendall	+3hrs 30min	Ulmarra	+4hrs 30min
Kiama	0	Wardell	+1 hr 30 min
Kurnell	0	Watson Taylors Lake	+2hrs
Lismore	+1hr 15min	Wauchope	+1hr 30min
Liverpool+	+2hrs 30min	Windsor	+5hrs 50min
Lower Portland Ferry	+3hrs 5min	Wingham	+3hrs 15min
Lugarno	+1hr	Wisemans Ferry	+2hrs 15min
Maclean	+2hrs 15min	Wollomba River mouth	+1hr 50min
Merimbula Lake Bridge	+1hr 30min	Wollongong	0
Milperra	+2hrs 10min	Wooli	+1hr 5min

Day	Date		Tide 1	
Wed	1		3:07 AM	(1.09) H
THu	2		4:18 AM	(1.15) H
Fri	3		5:10 AM	(1.24) H
Sat	4		5:53 AM	(1.36) H
Sun	5		12:29 AM	(0.31) L
Mon	6		2:05 AM	(0.24) L
Tue	7	○	2:43 AM	(0.21) L
Wed	8		3:22 AM	(0.22) L
THu	9		4:02 AM	(0.27) L
Fri	10		4:45 AM	(0.36) L
Sat	11		5:32 AM	(0.46) L
Sun	12		12:51 AM	(1.29) H
Mon	13		2:00 AM	(1.20) H
Tue	14		3:22 AM	(1.16) H
Wed	15		4:39 AM	(1.20) H
THu	16		5:41 AM	(1.27) H
Fri	17		12:20 AM	(0.44) L
Sat	18		1:00 AM	(0.42) L
Sun	19		1:34 AM	(0.41) L
Mon	20		2:04 AM	(0.41) L
Tue	21	●	2:32 AM	(0.43) L
Wed	22		3:00 AM	(0.45) L
THu	23		3:28 AM	(0.49) L
Fri	24		3:57 AM	(0.54) L
Sat	25		4:29 AM	(0.59) L
Sun	26		5:04 AM	(0.64) L
Mon	27		12:24 AM	(1.19) H
Tue	28		1:15 AM	(1.15) H
Wed	29		2:17 AM	(1.13) H
THu	30		3:29 AM	(1.15) H
Fri	31		4:34 AM	(1.23) H

OCTOBER 2025

Tide 2			Tide 3			Tide 4		
8:25 AM	(0.78)	L	3:10 PM	(1.46)	H	10:19 PM	(0.59)	L
9:40 AM	(0.73)	L	4:16 PM	(1.52)	H	11:09 PM	(0.49)	L
10:43 AM	(0.64)	L	5:10 PM	(1.61)	H	11:51 PM	(0.40)	L
11:36 AM	(0.53)	L	5:57 PM	(1.70)	H			
7:33 AM	(1.49)	H	1:25 PM	(0.42)	L	7:42 PM	(1.76)	
8:14 AM	(1.63)	H	2:14 PM	(0.32)	L	8:27 PM	(1.77)	H
8:55 AM	(1.75)	H	3:04 PM	(0.25)	L	9:14 PM	(1.74)	H
9:39 AM	(1.85)	H	3:56 PM	(0.21)	L	10:02 PM	(1.66)	H
10:24 AM	(1.90)	H	4:50 PM	(0.21)	L	10:55 PM	(1.54)	H
11:13 AM	(1.91)	H	5:47 PM	(0.25)	L	11:50 PM	(1.41)	H
12:03 PM	(1.86)	H	6:50 PM	(0.33)	L			
6:25 AM	(0.57)	L	1:00 PM	(1.78)	H	8:00 PM	(0.40)	L
7:28 AM	(0.66)	L	2:05 PM	(1.69)	H	9:17 PM	(0.46)	L
8:42 AM	(0.71)	L	3:19 PM	(1.62)	H	10:30 PM	(0.47)	L
10:02 AM	(0.71)	L	4:35 PM	(1.59)	H	11:31 PM	(0.46)	L
11:15 AM	(0.66)	L	5:39 PM	(1.58)	H			
6:29 AM	(1.36)	H	12:15 PM	(0.59)	L	6:31 PM	(1.58)	H
7:11 AM	(1.45)	H	1:07 PM	(0.53)	L	7:15 PM	(1.57)	H
7:47 AM	(1.53)	H	1:51 PM	(0.49)	L	7:54 PM	(1.54)	H
8:21 AM	(1.59)	H	2:32 PM	(0.45)	L	8:30 PM	(1.50)	H
8:53 AM	(1.65)	H	3:10 PM	(0.43)	L	9:07 PM	(1.46)	H
9:24 AM	(1.68)	H	3:47 PM	(0.42)	L	9:43 PM	(1.41)	H
9:56 AM	(1.70)	H	4:24 PM	(0.43)	L	10:19 PM	(1.36)	H
10:29 AM	(1.70)	H	5:02 PM	(0.45)	L	10:58 PM	(1.30)	H
11:03 AM	(1.68)	H	5:44 PM	(0.49)	L	11:39 PM	(1.25)	H
11:41 AM	(1.64)	H	6:29 PM	(0.53)	L			
5:45 AM	(0.69)	L	12:24 PM	(1.59)	H	7:20 PM	(0.58)	L
6:33 AM	(0.74)	L	1:14 PM	(1.53)	H	8:20 PM	(0.60)	L
7:34 AM	(0.78)	L	2:13 PM	(1.50)	H	9:26 PM	(0.59)	L
8:47 AM	(0.78)	L	3:20 PM	(1.49)	H	10:25 PM	(0.54)	L
10:01 AM	(0.74)	L	4:28 PM	(1.52)	H	11:16 PM	(0.47)	L

SOLAR/LUNAR BITE TIMES

Apogee moon phase on Friday 24th

Perigee moon phase on Wednesday 8th

● **New moon on Tuesday 21st**

First quarter moon on Thursday 30th

○ **Full moon on Tuesday 7th**

Last quarter moon phase on Tuesday 14th

Sydney, NSW: Rise: 06:13am Set: 07:08pm

Note: Daylight Savings start (clocks turn forward 1 hour) on Sunday, October 5th at 2:00 AM.

Subtract 1 hour to rise/set time for days before October 1st. These sun rise/set times are averages for the month

DAY	MINOR BITE	MAJOR BITE	MINOR BITE	MAJOR BITE	SALT WATER RATING	FRESH WATER RATING
WED 1	10:42 AM	6:28 PM	1:24 AM	6:01 AM	5	6
THUR 2	11:48 AM	7:19 PM	2:05 AM	6:53 AM	4	5
FRI 3	12:57 PM	8:09 PM	2:40 AM	7:44 AM	3	5
SAT 4	2:07 PM	8:58 PM	3:10 AM	8:33 AM	6	6
SUN 5	3:17 PM	9:47 PM	3:38 AM	9:22 AM	5	7
MON 6	4:30 PM	10:36 PM	4:04 AM	10:11 AM	3	8
TUE 7	5:44 PM	11:27 PM	4:30 AM	11:01 AM	○ 5	7
WED 8	7:01 PM		4:59 AM	11:54 AM	7	6
THUR 9	8:21 PM	12:21 AM	5:31 AM	12:50 PM	7	6
FRI 10	9:39 PM	1:19 AM	6:10 AM	1:50 PM	5	5
SAT 11	10:53 PM	2:21 AM	6:58 AM	2:52 PM	4	4

POPULAR LOCATION ADJUSTMENTS (See full list on page 7)

DAY	MINOR BITE	MAJOR BITE	MINOR BITE	MAJOR BITE	SALT WATER RATING	FRESH WATER RATING
UN 12	11:57 PM	3:25 AM	7:55 AM	3:56 PM	3	6
MON 13		4:28 AM	9:01 AM	4:57 PM	4	4
UE 14	12:48 AM	5:27 AM	10:11 AM	5:54 PM	5	5
WED 15	1:30 AM	6:22 AM	11:21 AM	6:47 PM	6	6
THUR 16	2:03 AM	7:12 AM	12:29 PM	7:34 PM	7	7
RI 17	2:30 AM	7:58 AM	1:34 PM	8:18 PM	7	8
SAT 18	2:54 AM	8:40 AM	2:35 PM	9:00 PM	5	8
SUN 19	3:16 AM	9:21 AM	3:36 PM	9:41 PM	6	7
MON 20	3:37 AM	10:01 AM	4:35 PM	10:21 PM	8	8
TUE 21	3:59 AM	10:42 AM	5:35 PM	11:03 PM ●	8	8
WED 22	4:23 AM	11:24 AM	6:35 PM	11:45 PM	8	8
THUR 23	4:49 AM	12:08 PM	7:36 PM		8	6
FRI 24	5:20 AM	12:55 PM	8:37 PM	12:31 AM	7	6
SAT 25	5:57 AM	1:44 PM	9:36 PM	1:19 AM	6	7
SUN 26	6:41 AM	2:35 PM	10:31 PM	2:09 AM	5	5
MON 27	7:32 AM	3:27 PM	11:19 PM	3:00 AM	4	6
TUE 28	8:30 AM	4:19 PM		3:53 AM	3	5
WED 29	9:33 AM	5:10 PM	12:01 AM	4:44 AM	3	5
THUR 30	10:39 AM	5:59 PM	12:37 AM	5:34 AM	4	6
FRI 31	11:46 AM	6:47 PM	1:08 AM	6:23 AM	5	6

TIDE TIMES

Tim Smith's

POPULAR TIDE ADJUSTMENTS

Ballina Boat Dock	+15min	Morpeth	+3hrs 10min
Batemans Bay	-1min	Moruya	+30min
Bermagui	+5min	Murwillumbah	+2hrs 30min
Blackmans Point	+1hr 15min	Narooma	+40min
Botany Bay	+3min	Nelson Bay	+30min
Broughton Island	-6min	Peats Ferry Bridge	+1hr
Byron Bay	0	Pindimar	+45min
Chinderah	+1hr 15min	Pittwater Entrance	0
Clyde River Bridge	+15min	Port Hacking	+2min
Coffs Harbour	-2min	Port Hacking Audley	+30min
Como	+30min	Port Hacking Burraneer	+15min
Coraki	+4hrs	Port Hacking Lilli Pilli	+30min
Crookhaven Jetty	+15min	Port Macquarie	+21min
Crowdy Head	0	Port Stephens	0
Danger Island	+18min	Queens Lake	+2hrs
Dolls Point	+15min	Raleigh	+1hr
Ettalong	+30min	Raymond Terrace	+1hr 55min
Evans Head Bridge	0	Salamander Bay	+45min
Fig Tree Bridge	+15min	Sandon	+30min
Forster	+1min	Shoalhaven Riv' Nowra	+2hrs 10min
Gabo Island	-9min	Shoalhaven Riv'O'Keefes Pt	+2hrs
Gladesville Bridge	+15min	Silverwater Bridge	+15min
Gladstone	+2hrs 10min	Soldiers Point	+1hr
Grafton	+4hrs 1 min	South West Rocks	+1hr 2min
Greenwell Point	+45min	Swansea	-3min
Harrington	+1 min	Taree	+2hrs
Harrington Inlet	+16min	Tea Gardens	+1hr
Hexham	+1hr 10min	Terranora Inlet	+2hrs 10min
Huskisson	+3min	The Spit Bridge	0
Iluka	0	Trial Bay	0
Jervis Bay	-3min	Tweed Heads	+4min
Kempsey	+3hrs 15min	Ulladulla Harbour	0
Kendall	+3hrs 30min	Ulmarra	+4hrs 30min
Kiama	0	Wardell	+1 hr 30 min
Kurnell	0	Watson Taylors Lake	+2hrs
Lismore	+1hr 15min	Wauchope	+1hr 30min
Liverpool+	+2hrs 30min	Windsor	+5hrs 50min
Lower Portland Ferry	+3hrs 5min	Wingham	+3hrs 15min
Lugarno	+1hr	Wisemans Ferry	+2hrs 15min
Maclean	+2hrs 15min	Wollomba River mouth	+1hr 50min
Merimbula Lake Bridge	+1hr 30min	Wollongong	0
Milperra	+2hrs 10min	Wooli	+1hr 5min

Fort Denison

Day	Date		Tide 1	
Sat	1		5:28 AM	(1.34) **H**
Sun	2		12:00 AM	(0.39) L
Mon	3		12:42 AM	(0.33) L
Tue	4		1:23 AM	(0.29) L
Wed	5	○	2:04 AM	(0.29) L
THu	6		2:47 AM	(0.32) L
Fri	7		3:33 AM	(0.37) L
Sat	8		4:22 AM	(0.44) L
Sun	9		5:15 AM	(0.52) L
Mon	10		12:45 AM	(1.28) **H**
Tue	11		1:51 AM	(1.24) **H**
Wed	12		3:00 AM	(1.24) **H**
THu	13		4:06 AM	(1.28) **H**
Fri	14		5:03 AM	(1.34) **H**
Sat	15		5:52 AM	(1.42) **H**
Sun	16		12:11 AM	(0.51) L
Mon	17		12:45 AM	(0.51) L
Tue	18		1:17 AM	(0.51) L
Wed	19		1:49 AM	(0.52) L
THu	20	●	2:21 AM	(0.54) L
Fri	21		2:53 AM	(0.56) L
Sat	22		3:28 AM	(0.59) L
Sun	23		4:04 AM	(0.62) L
Mon	24		4:44 AM	(0.65) L
Tue	25		12:06 AM	(1.23) **H**
Wed	26		12:55 AM	(1.21) **H**
THu	27		1:48 AM	(1.22) **H**
Fri	28		2:48 AM	(1.25) **H**
Sat	29		3:48 AM	(1.33) **H**
Sun	30		4:44 AM	(1.44) **H**

Tide 2		Tide 3		Tide 4	
11:09 AM	(0.66) L	5:27 PM	(1.57) H		
6:15 AM	(1.48) H	12:10 PM	(0.55) L	6:20 PM	(1.62) H
6:59 AM	(1.63) H	1:06 PM	(0.42) L	7:12 PM	(1.64) H
7:42 AM	(1.78) H	2:00 PM	(0.31) L	8:02 PM	(1.63) H
8:28 AM	(1.90) H	2:54 PM	(0.22) L	8:56 PM	(1.59) H
9:15 AM	(1.99) H	3:48 PM	(0.18) L	9:50 PM	(1.52) H
10:03 AM	(2.03) H	4:45 PM	(0.17) L	10:46 PM	(1.44) H
10:54 AM	(2.01) H	5:42 PM	(0.21) L	11:45 PM	(1.35) H
11:48 AM	(1.95) H	6:44 PM	(0.28) L		
6:12 AM	(0.60) L	12:45 PM	(1.84) H	7:47 PM	(0.36) L
7:15 AM	(0.67) L	1:45 PM	(1.73) H	8:52 PM	(0.43) L
8:25 AM	(0.71) L	2:52 PM	(1.62) H	9:53 PM	(0.48) L
9:38 AM	(0.72) L	3:59 PM	(1.53) H	10:46 PM	(0.50) L
10:49 AM	(0.71) L	5:00 PM	(1.47) H	11:31 PM	(0.51) L
11:53 AM	(0.66) L	5:54 PM	(1.43) H		
6:35 AM	(1.51) H	12:48 PM	(0.61) L	6:41 PM	(1.40) H
7:13 AM	(1.59) H	1:35 PM	(0.56) L	7:24 PM	(1.38) H
7:48 AM	(1.65) H	2:16 PM	(0.51) L	8:04 PM	(1.36) H
8:21 AM	(1.71) H	2:55 PM	(0.46) L	8:44 PM	(1.34) H
8:55 AM	(1.74) H	3:32 PM	(0.43) L	9:23 PM	(1.32) H
9:29 AM	(1.76) H	4:10 PM	(0.42) L	10:02 PM	(1.30) H
10:04 AM	(1.77) H	4:47 PM	(0.43) L	10:42 PM	(1.28) H
10:41 AM	(1.75) H	5:28 PM	(0.45) L	11:23 PM	(1.25) H
11:20 AM	(1.72) H	6:10 PM	(0.49) L		
5:26 AM	(0.68) L	12:01 PM	(1.68) H	6:56 PM	(0.51) L
6:14 AM	(0.71) L	12:47 PM	(1.63) H	7:46 PM	(0.53) L
7:10 AM	(0.74) L	1:38 PM	(1.58) H	8:38 PM	(0.52) L
8:15 AM	(0.75) L	2:35 PM	(1.54) H	9:30 PM	(0.50) L
9:25 AM	(0.73) L	3:39 PM	(1.51) H	10:21 PM	(0.46) L
10:37 AM	(0.67) L	4:45 PM	(1.50) H	11:10 PM	(0.43) L

SOLAR/LUNAR BITE TIMES

Tim Smith's

Apogee moon phase on Thursday 20th
Perigee moon phase on Thursday 6th
● **New moon on Thursday 20th**
First quarter moon on Friday 28th
○ **Full moon on Wednesday 5th**
Last quarter moon phase on Wednesday 12th

Sydney, NSW: Rise: 05:40am Set: 07:30pm
(Note: These sun rise/set times are averages for the month)

DAY	MINOR BITE	MAJOR BITE	MINOR BITE	MAJOR BITE	SALT WATER RATING	FRESH WATER RATING
SAT 1	12:54 PM	7:34 PM	1:36 AM	7:10 AM	4	5
SUN 2	2:04 PM	8:21 PM	2:02 AM	7:57 AM	3	5
MON 3	3:16 PM	9:11 PM	2:28 AM	8:46 AM	6	6
TUE 4	4:31 PM	10:03 PM	2:55 AM	9:37 AM	3	8
WED 5	5:50 PM	11:00 PM	3:25 AM	10:31 AM	○ 5	7
THUR 6	7:12 PM		4:01 AM	11:31 AM	7	6
FRI 7	8:31 PM	12:02 AM	4:46 AM	12:34 PM	7	6
SAT 8	9:42 PM	1:07 AM	5:41 AM	1:39 PM	5	5
SUN 9	10:41 PM	2:13 AM	6:46 AM	2:45 PM	4	4
MON 10	11:27 PM	3:17 AM	7:57 AM	3:46 PM	3	6
TUE 11		4:16 AM	9:10 AM	4:41 PM	4	4

NOVEMBER 2025

POPULAR LOCATION ADJUSTMENTS (See full list on page 7)

DAY	MINOR BITE	MAJOR BITE	MINOR BITE	MAJOR BITE	SALT WATER RATING	FRESH WATER RATING
WED 12	12:04 AM	5:08 AM	10:20 AM	5:32 PM	5	5
THUR 13	12:33 AM	5:56 AM	11:27 AM	6:18 PM	6	6
FRI 14	12:59 AM	6:40 AM	12:29 PM	7:00 PM	7	7
SAT 15	1:21 AM	7:21 AM	1:30 PM	7:41 PM	7	7
SUN 16	1:42 AM	8:01 AM	2:29 PM	8:21 PM	7	8
MON 17	2:04 AM	8:41 AM	3:28 PM	9:01 PM	5	8
TUE 18	2:27 AM	9:22 AM	4:28 PM	9:44 PM	6	7
WED 19	2:53 AM	10:06 AM	5:29 PM	10:29 PM	8	8
THUR 20	3:22 AM	10:52 AM	6:30 PM	11:15 PM ●	8	8
FRI 21	3:57 AM	11:40 AM	7:29 PM		8	6
SAT 22	4:39 AM	12:31 PM	8:25 PM	12:05 AM	7	6
SUN 23	5:28 AM	1:23 PM	9:16 PM	12:57 AM	7	6
MON 24	6:24 AM	2:15 PM	10:00 PM	1:49 AM	6	7
TUE 25	7:25 AM	3:05 PM	10:37 PM	2:39 AM	5	5
WED 26	8:29 AM	3:54 PM	11:09 PM	3:29 AM	4	6
THUR 27	9:34 AM	4:41 PM	11:37 PM	4:17 AM	3	5
FRI 28	10:39 AM	5:26 PM		5:03 AM	4	6
SAT 29	11:46 AM	6:12 PM	12:02 AM	5:48 AM	5	6
SUN 30	12:54 PM	6:58 PM	12:27 AM	6:34 AM	4	5

TIDE TIMES

Tim Smith's

POPULAR TIDE ADJUSTMENTS

Ballina Boat Dock	+15min	Morpeth	+3hrs 10min
Batemans Bay	-1min	Moruya	+30min
Bermagui	+5min	Murwillumbah	+2hrs 30min
Blackmans Point	+1hr 15min	Narooma	+40min
Botany Bay	+3min	Nelson Bay	+30min
Broughton Island	-6min	Peats Ferry Bridge	+1hr
Byron Bay	0	Pindimar	+45min
Chinderah	+1hr 15min	Pittwater Entrance	0
Clyde River Bridge	+15min	Port Hacking	+2min
Coffs Harbour	-2min	Port Hacking Audley	+ 30min
Como	+30min	Port Hacking Burraneer	+15min
Coraki	+4hrs	Port Hacking Lilli Pilli	+30min
Crookhaven Jetty	+15min	Port Macquarie	+21min
Crowdy Head	0	Port Stephens	0
Danger Island	+18min	Queens Lake	+2hrs
Dolls Point	+15min	Raleigh	+1hr
Ettalong	+30min	Raymond Terrace	+1hr 55min
Evans Head Bridge	0	Salamander Bay	+45min
Fig Tree Bridge	+15min	Sandon	+30min
Forster	+1min	Shoalhaven Riv' Nowra	+2hrs 10min
Gabo Island	-9min	Shoalhaven Riv'O'Keefes Pt	+2hrs
Gladesville Bridge	+15min	Silverwater Bridge	+15min
Gladstone	+2hrs 10min	Soldiers Point	+1hr
Grafton	+4hrs 1 min	South West Rocks	+1hr 2min
Greenwell Point	+45min	Swansea	-3min
Harrington	+1 min	Taree	+2hrs
Harrington Inlet	+16min	Tea Gardens	+1hr
Hexham	+1hr 10min	Terranora Inlet	+2hrs 10min
Huskisson	+3min	The Spit Bridge	0
Iluka	0	Trial Bay	0
Jervis Bay	-3min	Tweed Heads	+4min
Kempsey	+3hrs 15min	Ulladulla Harbour	0
Kendall	+3hrs 30min	Ulmarra	+4hrs 30min
Kiama	0	Wardell	+1 hr 30 min
Kurnell	0	Watson Taylors Lake	+2hrs
Lismore	+1hr 15min	Wauchope	+1hr 30min
Liverpool+	+2hrs 30min	Windsor	+5hrs 50min
Lower Portland Ferry	+3hrs 5min	Wingham	+3hrs 15min
Lugarno	+1hr	Wisemans Ferry	+2hrs 15min
Maclean	+2hrs 15min	Wollomba River mouth	+1hr 50min
Merimbula Lake Bridge	+1hr 30min	Wollongong	0
Milperra	+2hrs 10min	Wooli	+1hr 5min

Fort Denison

Day	Date	Tide 1	
Mon	1	5:35 AM	(1.58) H
Tue	2	6:25 AM	(1.73) H
Wed	3	12:45 AM	(0.39) L
THu	4	1:32 AM	(0.39) L
Fri	5	2:23 AM	(0.41) L
Sat	6	3:14 AM	(0.44) L
Sun	7	4:07 AM	(0.47) L
Mon	8	5:02 AM	(0.52) L
Tue	9	12:29 AM	(1.33) H
Wed	10	1:26 AM	(1.32) H
THu	11	2:23 AM	(1.32) H
Fri	12	3:19 AM	(1.34) H
Sat	13	4:15 AM	(1.39) H
Sun	14	5:06 AM	(1.46) H
Mon	15	5:53 AM	(1.52) H
Tue	16	6:36 AM	(1.59) H
Wed	17	12:35 AM	(0.60) L
THu	18	1:15 AM	(0.60) L
Fri	19	1:53 AM	(0.60) L
Sat	20	2:31 AM	(0.60) L
Sun	21	3:10 AM	(0.59) L
Mon	22	3:49 AM	(0.59) L
Tue	23	4:30 AM	(0.60) L
Wed	24	5:12 AM	(0.61) L
THu	25	12:30 AM	(1.31) H
Fri	26	1:18 AM	(1.33) H
Sat	27	2:10 AM	(1.37) H
Sun	28	3:05 AM	(1.44) H
Mon	29	4:02 AM	(1.53) H
Tue	30	5:00 AM	(1.64) H
Wed	31	5:59 AM	(1.76) H

DECEMBER 2025

Tide 2		Tide 3		Tide 4	
11:46 AM	(0.57) L	5:47 PM	(1.49) H	11:57 PM	(0.40) L
12:50 PM	(0.45) L	6:47 PM	(1.48) H		
7:15 AM	(1.87) H	1:50 PM	(0.33) L	7:46 PM	(1.47) H
8:05 AM	(1.98) H	2:47 PM	(0.24) L	8:45 PM	(1.45) H
8:57 AM	(2.05) H	3:44 PM	(0.18) L	9:42 PM	(1.42) H
9:49 AM	(2.08) H	4:38 PM	(0.17) L	10:38 PM	(1.39) H
10:42 AM	(2.06) H	5:32 PM	(0.20) L	11:33 PM	(1.36) H
11:34 AM	(1.98) H	6:27 PM	(0.27) L		
5:59 AM	(0.57) L	12:27 PM	(1.87) H	7:20 PM	(0.35) L
6:56 AM	(0.63) L	1:19 PM	(1.73) H	8:13 PM	(0.43) L
7:57 AM	(0.69) L	2:13 PM	(1.59) H	9:01 PM	(0.50) L
9:01 AM	(0.74) L	3:09 PM	(1.46) H	9:47 PM	(0.55) L
10:12 AM	(0.75) L	4:08 PM	(1.35) H	10:31 PM	(0.58) L
11:20 AM	(0.74) L	5:07 PM	(1.28) H	11:14 PM	(0.59) L
12:24 PM	(0.69) L	6:03 PM	(1.25) H	11:55 PM	(0.60) L
1:16 PM	(0.62) L	6:56 PM	(1.24) H		
7:16 AM	(1.65) H	2:01 PM	(0.55) L	7:44 PM	(1.25) H
7:55 AM	(1.71) H	2:41 PM	(0.49) L	8:27 PM	(1.27) H
8:32 AM	(1.75) H	3:19 PM	(0.45) L	9:07 PM	(1.28) H
9:10 AM	(1.78) H	3:56 PM	(0.42) L	9:46 PM	(1.29) H
9:47 AM	(1.80) H	4:32 PM	(0.41) L	10:25 PM	(1.29) H
10:25 AM	(1.81) H	5:11 PM	(0.41) L	11:04 PM	(1.29) H
11:03 AM	(1.79) H	5:49 PM	(0.42) L	11:45 PM	(1.29) H
11:43 AM	(1.76) H	6:30 PM	(0.43) L		
5:58 AM	(0.64) L	12:24 PM	(1.71) H	7:11 PM	(0.44) L
6:50 AM	(0.66) L	1:09 PM	(1.64) H	7:55 PM	(0.45) L
7:48 AM	(0.69) L	2:00 PM	(1.55) H	8:41 PM	(0.46) L
8:56 AM	(0.69) L	3:00 PM	(1.46) H	9:30 PM	(0.48) L
10:12 AM	(0.66) L	4:09 PM	(1.39) H	10:24 PM	(0.49) L
11:30 AM	(0.58) L	5:23 PM	(1.34) H	11:20 PM	(0.50) L
12:43 PM	(0.47) L	6:34 PM	(1.33) H		

SOLAR/LUNAR BITE TIMES

Tim Smith's

Apogee moon phase on Wednesday 17th
Perigee moon phase on Thursday 4th
● New moon on Satday 20th
First quarter moon on Sunday 28th
○ Full moon on Friday 5th
Last quarter moon phase on Friday 12th

Sydney, NSW: Rise: 05:30am Set: 08:00pm
(Note: These sun rise/set times are averages for the month)

DAY	MINOR BITE	MAJOR BITE	MINOR BITE	MAJOR BITE	SALT WATER RATING	FRESH WATER RATING
MON 1	2:04 PM	7:47 PM	12:52 AM	7:22 AM	3	5
TUE 2	3:19 PM	8:40 PM	1:20 AM	8:13 AM	6	6
WED 3	4:38 PM	9:39 PM	1:52 AM	9:09 AM	5	7
THUR 4	5:59 PM	10:43 PM	2:31 AM	10:11 AM	3	8
FRI 5	7:16 PM	11:50 PM	3:21 AM	11:16 AM	○ 5	7
SAT 6	8:23 PM		4:22 AM	12:23 PM	7	6
SUN 7	9:17 PM	12:57 AM	5:33 AM	1:28 PM	7	6
MON 8	10:00 PM	2:00 AM	6:49 AM	2:28 PM	5	5
TUE 9	10:33 PM	2:58 AM	8:03 AM	3:23 PM	4	4
WED 10	11:01 PM	3:49 AM	9:13 AM	4:12 PM	3	6
THUR 11	11:25 PM	4:36 AM	10:19 AM	4:57 PM	4	4

DAY	MINOR BITE	MAJOR BITE	MINOR BITE	MAJOR BITE	SALT WATER RATING	FRESH WATER RATING
FRI 12	11:47 PM	5:19 AM	11:22 AM	5:39 PM	5	5
SAT 13		6:00 AM	12:22 PM	6:19 PM	6	6
SUN 14	12:08 AM	6:40 AM	1:21 PM	7:00 PM	7	7
MON 15	12:31 AM	7:21 AM	2:21 PM	7:42 PM	7	8
TUE 16	12:56 AM	8:04 AM	3:21 PM	8:26 PM	5	8
WED 17	1:24 AM	8:49 AM	4:22 PM	9:12 PM	5	8
THUR 18	1:57 AM	9:36 AM	5:22 PM	10:01 PM	6	7
FRI 19	2:37 AM	10:27 AM	6:20 PM	10:52 PM	8	8
SAT 20	3:24 AM	11:19 AM	7:13 PM	11:45 PM ●	8	8
SUN 21	4:19 AM	12:11 PM	7:59 PM		8	8
MON 22	5:19 AM	1:02 PM	8:38 PM	12:36 AM	7	6
TUE 23	6:22 AM	1:52 PM	9:11 PM	1:26 AM	6	7
WED 24	7:27 AM	2:39 PM	9:40 PM	2:15 AM	5	5
THUR 25	8:32 AM	3:24 PM	10:06 PM	3:01 AM	4	6
FRI 26	9:37 AM	4:09 PM	10:30 PM	3:46 AM	4	6
SAT 27	10:42 AM	4:53 PM	10:54 PM	4:30 AM	3	5
SUN 28	11:49 AM	5:39 PM	11:19 PM	5:15 AM	4	6
MON 29	12:59 PM	6:28 PM	11:48 PM	6:03 AM	5	6
TUE 30	2:14 PM	7:22 PM		6:55 AM	4	5
WED 31	3:31 PM	8:21 PM	12:23 AM	7:51 AM	3	5

POPULAR RIGS

Saltwater Rigs

Surface Float Rig

An excellent surface salmon rig consists of a styrene float, a couple of 4/0 hooks and a small sinker for weight. The hooks are tied on a metre or so of 15 kg monofilament trace and are spaced to hold a full pilchard comfortably. Slip a running ball sinker down the trace right on to the top hook. Then slip on a running styrene float and attach the top of the trace to a good quality swivel. This will allow the float to suspend your bait at the correct depth for feeding salmon. Should you require the bait to be set deeper, simply extend the trace length.

This rig casts reasonably well from a threadline or sidecast outfit and can be modified easily to suit small or large salmon, tommy ruff, tailor (with the inclusion of a light wire trace) and trevally.

Glitterbug float

Sinker

3–6 kg fluorocarbon leader to bait

5 kg mono

Freshwater Rig

Standard Paternoster for Boat and Bank

This is a standard rig for many Australian native species from barra to cod, using anything from a worm, to a yabby, to a live bait or prawn for barra.

You can vary the length of the droppers, depending on conditions, and the 3-way swivel could be substituted with a brass ring if the fish encountered are likely to pull your arms off! Add a red bead too—it can add a touch of spark and get those fish biting.

Fixed teardrop sinker

POPULAR
KNOTS

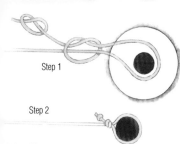

Step 1

Step 2

Arbor Knot

This is a very fast and secure knot for attaching line to the reel. Pass the tag end of the line around the spool and form an overhand knot with the tag end around the main line. Then another overhand knot on the tag end of the line. Lubricate the knots if using monofilament, tighten down by pulling the main line, and trim the tag.

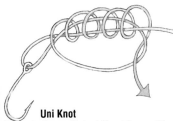

Uni Knot

An easy-to-tie versatile knot. Thread the eye of the hook with the line so the hook is suspended on a loop. Encircle the main line with the tag so another loop is formed. Wrap the double strand inside the loop with the tag. Make four wraps in all, leaving the tag protruding from the loop. Close the knot but do not pull it tight just yet. Slide the knot down onto the eye of the hook, pull it tight and trim the tag.

Homer Rhode Knot

This knot should never be used on lighter weight monofilaments, as it breaks at around 50 per cent of the line test.

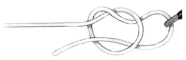

1. Form an overhand knot in the main line leaving approximately 20 cm (8 inches) of monofilament between the knot and the tag end. Pass the tag end through the hook eye and then back through the overhand knot from the same side as it exited. Tighten the overhand knot lightly to the hook eye by pulling on the tail of the hook and on the tag end of the line, while keeping the two lines parallel to prevent the hook from twisting on the knot.

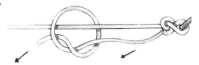

2. Make another overhand knot over the standing part of the line. This knot is the stopper for the loop, so its position determines the size of the loop, generally this knot would be 2–3 cm (1 inch) from the hook eye. Tighten this second knot and then pull on the bend of the hook and the main line at the same time.

3. The knot at the hook eye should slide up the line snugly into the second knot. Trim the tag.

Spider Hitch

This is an easy-to-tie and effective double line loop which is good for attaching small diameter lines to large diameter lines. Although quick to tie, it is not as effective as the Bimini Twist Knot.

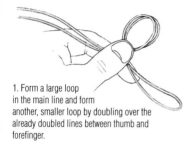

1. Form a large loop in the main line and form another, smaller loop by doubling over the already doubled lines between thumb and forefinger.

2. With the larger loop, take five or six wraps over the thumb starting at the base of the thumb and working forward. Pass the larger loop through the smaller loop at the end of the thumb and draw the loop through, pulling the coils off the thumb as you do so.

3. Lubricate the loose knot and tighten it by pulling on the main line and tag and the loop at the opposite end. Trim the tag.

Albright Knotz

The Albright knot serves to join two monofilament lines of different diameters, such as when attaching a heavier leader to your main line. DO NOT use the Albright to tie a mono leader to superbraid line because the knot may slip!

1. Form a loop in the end of the heavier line by bending back about 5 inches of line. Pass the tag end of the lighter line through this loop.

2. Pinch the lines about 3 inches from the end of the loop, leaving about 3 inches of tag beyond this point to tie the knot.

3. Working down toward the loop, take 10 wraps around all three strands of line. Pass the tag end through the end loop on the same side it originally entered.

4. Slowly pull both strands of lighter line while grasping the heavier line and working the knot's coils toward the loop end. Do not let the coils slip off the loop. Tighten, then trim the tag ends.

FISH
ID
N S W

AUSTRALIAN SALMON

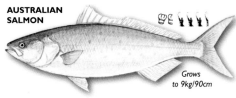

Grows to 9kg/90cm

BLACK BREAM

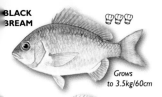

Grows to 3.5kg/60cm

YELLOWFIN BREAM

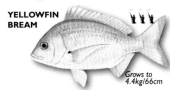

Grows to 4.4kg/66cm

TARWHINE
Min 20cm

Grows to 3kg/50cm

LUDERICK

Grows to 4.5kg/70cm

DUSKY FLATHEAD

Grows to 10kg/150cm

FLOUNDER

Grows to 1kg/50cm

GROPER (EASTERN BLUE)

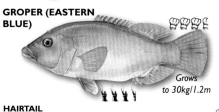

Grows to 30kg/1.2m

LEATHERJACKET

Grows to 35cm

HAIRTAIL

Grows to 6kg/235cm

Tim Smith's Tide and Fish Times - NSW

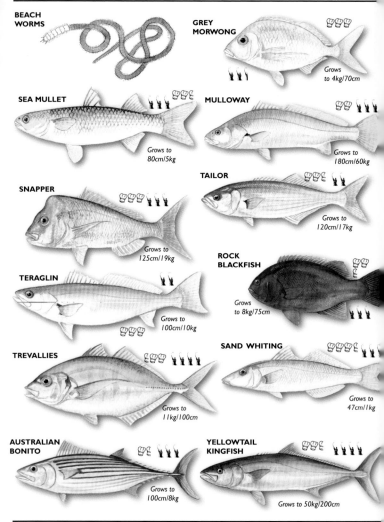

BEACH WORMS

GREY MORWONG

Grows to 4kg/70cm

SEA MULLET

Grows to 80cm/5kg

MULLOWAY

Grows to 180cm/60kg

SNAPPER

Grows to 125cm/19kg

TAILOR

Grows to 120cm/17kg

TERAGLIN

Grows to 100cm/10kg

ROCK BLACKFISH

Grows to 8kg/75cm

TREVALLIES

Grows to 11kg/100cm

SAND WHITING

Grows to 47cm/1kg

AUSTRALIAN BONITO

Grows to 100cm/8kg

YELLOWTAIL KINGFISH

Grows to 50kg/200cm

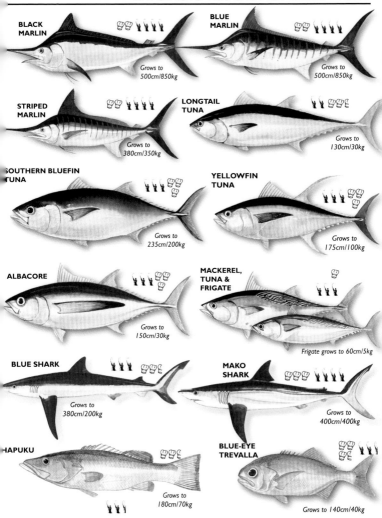

BLACK MARLIN

Grows to 500cm/850kg

BLUE MARLIN

Grows to 500cm/850kg

STRIPED MARLIN

Grows to 380cm/350kg

LONGTAIL TUNA

Grows to 130cm/30kg

SOUTHERN BLUEFIN TUNA

Grows to 235cm/200kg

YELLOWFIN TUNA

Grows to 175cm/100kg

ALBACORE

Grows to 150cm/30kg

MACKEREL, TUNA & FRIGATE

Frigate grows to 60cm/5kg

BLUE SHARK

Grows to 380cm/200kg

MAKO SHARK

Grows to 400cm/400kg

HAPUKU

Grows to 180cm/70kg

BLUE-EYE TREVALLA

Grows to 140cm/40kg

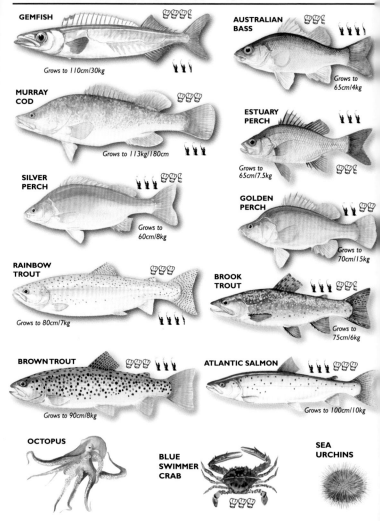

GEMFISH

Grows to 110cm/30kg

MURRAY COD

Grows to 113kg/180cm

SILVER PERCH

Grows to 60cm/8kg

RAINBOW TROUT

Grows to 80cm/7kg

BROWN TROUT

Grows to 90cm/8kg

AUSTRALIAN BASS

Grows to 65cm/4kg

ESTUARY PERCH

Grows to 65cm/7.5kg

GOLDEN PERCH

Grows to 70cm/15kg

BROOK TROUT

Grows to 75cm/6kg

ATLANTIC SALMON

Grows to 100cm/10kg

OCTOPUS

BLUE SWIMMER CRAB

SEA URCHINS

☠ DANGEROUS ☠ AND 🐟 POISONOUS 🐟 FISH

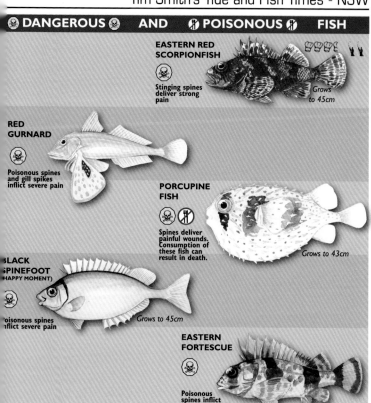

EASTERN RED SCORPIONFISH

Stinging spines deliver strong pain

Grows to 45cm

RED GURNARD

Poisonous spines and gill spikes inflict severe pain

PORCUPINE FISH

Spines deliver painful wounds. Consumption of these fish can result in death.

Grows to 43cm

BLACK SPINEFOOT
(HAPPY MOMENT)

Poisonous spines inflict severe pain

Grows to 45cm

EASTERN FORTESCUE

Poisonous spines inflict severe pain

LEGEND

 Poor Sport Fish

 Excellent Sport Fish

🍴 Poor Eating

🍴🍴🍴🍴 Excellent Eating

☠ Potentially dangerous

🚫 Not to be consumed

FISH COOLER DELUXE RANGE

Keep your catch
ICE COOL for **LONGER**

Small	915 mm x 460 mm x 300 mm	AC1136
Medium	1220 mm x 510 mm x 300 mm	AC1143
Large	1520 mm x 510 mm x 300 mm	AC1150
Extra Large	1830 mm x 510 mm x 300 mm	AC1167

Small

Medium

Large

Extra Large

KAYAK COOLER DELUXE RANGE

Medium	610 mm length - Top width 180mm - Bottom width x 400 mm	AC1112-11000
Large	910 mm length - Top width 250mm - Bottom width x 510 mm	AC1129-13700

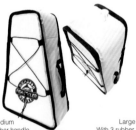

Medium
With rubber handle

Large
With 3 rubber handles